Bridge Over Niger

Department of State **TELEGRAM**

December 14, 1970

PAGE 01   STATE   203017

83
ORIGIN AF-19

INFO   OCT-01   CPR-02   PM-05   NSC-10   JL03   RSC-01   SS-20   USIA-12

PRS-01   /074 R

66634
DRAFTED BY: AF W CHTWINING
APPROVED BY: AF WWITMAN II
AF W MR. AGGREY
S CPR DMJOHNSON
S S MR. CURRAN
THE WHITE HOUSE MR. MARSHALL WRIGHT
----------------------   069852

R 142254Z DEC 70
FM SECSTATE WASHDC
TO AMEMBASSY NIAMEY

LIMITED OFFICIAL USE STATE 203017

SUBJECT: NATIONAL DAY MESSAGE

1. FOLLOWING IS TEXT PRESIDENT'S NATIONAL DAY MSG TO
PRESIDENT DIORI. QUOTE DEAR MR. PRESIDENT: AS YOUR
COUNTRY CELEBRATES THIS SIGNIFICANT NATIONAL DAY, ALLOW ME
TO EXPRESS MY CONGRATULATIONS AND THOSE OF THE GOVERNMENT
AND PEOPLE OF THE UNITED STATES. I HAVE BEEN IMPRESSED BY
YOUR COUNTRY'S DEVELOPMENT EFFORTS AND AM MOST PLEASED THAT
THE UNITED STATES HAS BEEN ABLE TO ASSIST WITH THE IMPORTANT BRIDGE
BEING DEDICATED ON THIS DAY. I WISH
YOU CONTINUED SUCCESS IN YOUR WISE LEADERSHIP OF THE REPUBLIC
OF NIGER, AND I HOPE THAT THE ALREADY CLOSE RELATIONS BETWEEN
OUR TWO COUNTRIES WILL CONTINUE TO BE
STRENGTHENED. RICHARD M. NIXON. UNQUOTE

2. AS DEPT INTENDS INCORPORATE MSG IN SHORT SPEECH
PRESIDENTIAL REPRESENTATIVE ABBOTT WILL MAKE AT BRIDGE
DEDICATION, MSG WILL NOT BE SENT PRES DIORI COMMERCIALLY. ROGERS

Bridge Over Niger

The True Story of the J. F. Kennedy Bridge

Remo Capra Bloise
In Collaboration with Pat Fahey

Writer's Showcase
New York Lincoln Shanghai

Bridge Over Niger
The True Story of the J. F. Kennedy Bridge

Writer's Showcase
an imprint of iUniverse, Inc.

For information address:
iUniverse, Inc.
2021 Pine Lake Road, Suite 100
Lincoln, NE 68512
www.iuniverse.com

ISBN: 0-595-00694-9

Printed in the United States of America

Dedication

To Patricia Ann Fahey, my dearest and forever friend, who inspired and convinced me to write this book.

In our long discussions about the bridge, her words, ideas and research, gave me the beginning without which I could have not continued.

My gratitude and indelible affection go to her for her inspiration and for her help in writing "Bridge Over Niger."

*   *   *

Patricia A. Fahey's work as a writer, has been published in the New York Daily News, The Wall Street Journal, Town and Country and other major publications.

Contents

Acknowledgements

My sincere thanks to Joanne Hart in Southampton for helping me remember the details of our meeting with Erich Kahler in Princeton.

My thanks to Richie Berlin for her enthusiasm.

I express my appreciation to Felix Ziffer for reading the manuscript and for his advice.

My thanks also to Ivan Obolensky for reading the first draft and for his advice.

My thanks to Natalie Tuckerman for her technical advice.

My thanks to Mimi Strong for her helpful information.

My thanks to Craig Kaizer for editing the manuscript.

My thanks to Lucy De Rosa at Sony Special Products for her help with the cover jacket.

Doctor E.L.P

At 12 noon, on May 14, 1970, I walked into the white cinder cement building at 12th Street and Fifth Avenue, New York City. That avenue at 12th Street spoke as if it were ringed with memories. Long before the cake-icing marble went on the building here, it had been a diamond center. Before that copper. And I don't have to mention that during the famous Repeal time, the neighborhood sloshed with whiskey. My purpose in being here that day was to meet Dr. E.L.P. (Dr. E. Lionel Pavlo) Consulting Engineer for the bridge that would span the Niger River in Niamey, West Africa. I would go to West Africa as control. The ambiance of the building today is very like in a war construction zone from the forties. A glance through the plexiglass mirrored wall directory put Dr. ELP (Consulting Engineers) on the Tower Suite. I stopped at the bank of twin elevators to pull down the hidden gauze linen in the back of my lapel suit. Done discreetly of course, this small action. At the same time, I looked over to the doorman and gave my glasseyed wink. If you know that the first trick hand always lies hidden in the first play of a dice table, then you will understand why my mind is a storehouse of facts, like a casino boy's, who calls out the sides or plays from memory. Once inside the elevator, I always immediately check the metal casing of the doors only to find out who rods the wheels of the management of a building where I'm visiting. Occasionally, you have to get out fast. I say this wryly.

Straight to the front of my jacket came an unbearable heat as I rode up to Dr. ELP along with the strong smell of naphtha, probably used a few minutes before on the elevator floor carpet. But in spite of all these things, and I always say this to amuse myself, I began humming a current popular song to suit my good mood.

Through this ambiance of heat, steel, and naphtha, the door opened to Dr. ELP's reception area, center stage, straight line direct to both elevator cages, which means that Dr. ELP is the only one on the floor. A framed photograph of proportion 48" by 72" of the Golden Gate Bridge in San Francisco spans the entire reception area.

And this image spills over. Around the Golden Gate Bridge, hanging like a centerfold, were blown-up magazine covers. The one on the same side as the bridge photo was a profile side shot of Dr. ELP from Engineering News.

Somewhere, too, among all those feature articles and cover stories on Dr. ELP was a paragraph or so that says: "Dr. ELP came from Russia in his early years and calculated the tower measurements of the Golden Gate Bridge, San-Francisco." This is the first entry of the Dr. ELP story. And obviously, an important fact to remember.

This meeting with Dr. ELP is necessary because I was going to Niamey, West Africa to complete a bridge over the Niger River as the Resident Engineer. I am control. I was on a mission, and all missions are dangerous by definition. Especially when more than one government was involved and the project is classified American AID and the project had been stalled for over 5 years.

In line with the governmental booking on this project, Dr. ELP's offices are bugged probably to the point of twigging the wires over the air conditioner vents. Possibly one hot wire over another, in line with a general audience microphone. Under the Golden Gate Bridge Panorama span-photo sits Dr. ELP's receptionist, who, after hearing my name, presses the button for the back. Then, from under the spot light that discreetly marks the entrance to Dr. ELP's part of the floor, comes the charming voice of a slim lady welcoming me with, "I'm Susan, Dr. ELP's secretary."

It would take me close to a minute to get to Dr. ELP's office. I knew the time measurement here because I always count as to keep a record in my memory bank of important distances.

There was no chit-chat from Susan, since in D.C. the bridge was weight, which meant already the heads were flying all over the place. In fact the sweat was on D.C. like a heavy veneer

45 seconds brought me to an open door, face to face with Dr. ELP. Fast living has taught me to concentrate on the skull of the person I'm about to shake hands with, and forget about the background. If there's more than one body in the room, you can still play it hard, three to the hand, if you have the right overcoat in your hand. I'm big on self-defense, because sometimes you make an important appointment and the wrong guy appears.

Fortunately, the body in front of me was really Dr. ELP. I make it a point to know what my new friends look like before I visit them. After all, I would be representing Dr. ELP in Africa.

Dr. ELP was tall, which meant towering, over six feet. His face showed strong features and he had a groomed set of dark hair. There was a brilliance in his eyes and one would immediately know that he was very intelligent. His shoulders were large. He wore a well tailored gray suit, probably from Dunhill in NY and a white handkerchief in his small left pocket. He had a well pressed white shirt and a conservative tie. The knot of his tie was perfect. He wore black shoes, and most likely from England. And this list of gentlemanly worldly requirements goes on.

Susan made the official introduction: " Dr. ELP, may I present Mr. Remo Capra Bloise."

From the diplomatic point of view, which means government, the time of my official diplomatic standing, that official recognition by way of introduction, as required by regulation, was important: 12:07 P.M. EST.

These crucial moments of statecraft completed, Susan exited as efficiently as she had entered. Those words of introduction, if you know the meaning, were like a stop in the motion of time. Even so, my eyes had absorbed the entire woodwork of Dr. ELP's office.

For those who like grass-skirts, as I always say, or need mention of the decorative side of a man's office, Dr. ELP's office would not let the observer down. The vantage point is global: degrees from all the best engineering universities, like MIT. And professional engineering licenses from every state in the United States. That's the wall paper in Dr. ELP's office, including the ultra modern design for the internationally well known suspension bridge for the Straits of Messina in Sicily, Italy, for which he will receive later the first world-prize for its design.

Dr. ELP knew I knew a lot about him, and Dr. ELP would like to think he knew everything about me. In particular, I was well acquainted with many of Dr. ELP's friends, where the term "friend" has the complete meaning of sacrosanct. Thus, the talk went evenly and smoothly. We both knew what we were saying about that area. As it's said in Langley, Virginia, unless something positive is done, they are going to bring you back to D.C. in a casket.

In fact Dr. ELP knew in a very familiar way the very people in charge of that world zone and who approached me here in New York and invited me to take the Niger assignment. There's nothing vague about me or my background or my assignment. In the heavy construction industry, the phrase goes what is the outside fender on a specific job meaning what's the job requirement, as it's actually said on the management-side, because "Control" is a very big job. In this case, there are 3: Control must be a bridge engineer; he must be fluent in french, which I am, since I completed my initial study at Pascal-Michaut-Mongenast in Brussels, Belgium; and must have diplomatic experience, which I do as far back as Venezuela and its Ministry of agriculture. As a plus, the experience in pre-stressed concrete beams, which I gained from the approaches of the Narraganset Bay suspension bridge in Newport, Rhode Island, fit perfectly here. In fact, my background is so positive that to Dr. ELP's computer-zoned mind, I am like a heavy oil that greases well a machine.

At one point, Dr. ELP smiled and paused for a brief moment. I knew then and there that Dr. ELP liked me.

We had been conversing, of course in French. On Dr. ELP's part, "Monsieur...et bien, Remo...and then the heavy French phrases of a technical language, falling like steel.

To illustrate the delicacies, Dr. ELP reached over to a bronzed ash tray to grasp a pair of moulten balls like steel which, with his hands, DR. ELP moulds until the edge of the balls have became flattened like a knife. Regardless of Dr. ELP's intent, the symbolism lingers.

Nor are there any useless gestures in these soft movements of Dr. ELP's hands, where each muscle chord is as febrile yet unyielding as the kinks of steel. "Each mistake in this AID project has been costly" he said. "For the Americans." "They believe there's a possibility of sabotage." After pausing, Dr. ELP continued, "I know it's definite." In short, Dr.ELP added: "The American State Department now looks for a political solution to various problems."

"I've even been told, so to speak, to think the way they want me to" Dr. ELP says. "The razor sharp mind of one of the guys from the African desk in D.C., who likes to edit me if he can and who recently left my office here with these words:

1.) Niger is at this point a very strategic point in West Africa. We cannot afford to lose it.

2.) This bridge has to be completed by December 18, 1970 because of the election of President Diori, who's on the American side. The bridge will help develop the other side of Niamey with universities and other facilities for the advancement in education for the people of Niger.

3.) This is an American bridge, American in design and of American material of which 80% of the work has to be performed by American personnel and of American material."

At this 10-minute point of the meeting, the call from Washington, D.C. that both Dr. ELP and I expect is rung in. I am to leave for Niger via Paris or Rome immediately.

A choice of via *Paris or Rome* brought a wry smile to my face. It made me remember a friend in Europe who once described superbly, as a joke, a dish of choice renowned at the Hotel George Cinc in Paris. "Chicken a la Kiev", with the butter squirted either from the right outside of the chicken breast, for "*Paree*"; or squirted with superb touch to the center breast, several decimeters from the placement of the chicken on the plate, for *Rome*.

Dr. ELP's face revealed no interest in the pleasurable past-times of Europe or as it's said in Paris, "in such a convivial joke."

Thus, I put the choice straight to him with "Via Paris." And then I add in a metered kind of tone: "There's only one way to Niger and that's through the French. And put my hotel choice down here as the south chamber rooms of the George Cinq."

Things were happening quickly now: my flight booking is 7:15 p.m., 707 jet, first class, Air France to Paris. The departure is Kennedy Airport, the third departure field. The small limousine, which meant only two steel backed bucket seats would soon be in front of Dr. ELP's office building for the straight ride to the airport. "There's no use," I told Dr. ELP, "in sitting around here for another tomorrow."

Part of my memory bank mentioned earlier that what keeps me counting the important distances is a mind that listens. It's not the only one with an ear on the throat. For example, a world gambler, who once spent a few years on the side of the construction world, said to me once: "Remo, let your mind count and your ears fix on the guy's words, that is, on his throat."

While Dr. ELP leaned on the credenza desk, reaching for one of the telephones, with his right arm raised slightly in the air, with calls coming in and out, to facilitate, one of Dr. ELP's favorite words, my departure, I, for the last time, asked myself, who is Dr. ELP in reality beyond the photos; press releases and world credits?

To my mind Dr. ELP was as shrewd and wise as the next old man. In my opinion, there isn't a pitiful bone in his body. And Dr. ELP knew what I knew: Africa is a rough terrain.

These closing thoughts of mine coincided with the entrance of Perry Huang, Dr. ELP's bridge designer. The introduction was made. I said goodbye to Dr. ELP then with these words: "A presto", which is a Italian for "I'll see you soon, I'll be in touch."

Perry Huang and I left Dr. ELP for a turn to the office behind Dr. ELP's. Perry's office was big and organized for work, like the front room of an oil refinery, the high-grade opposite to the full layout of Dr. ELP's. Within the ELP organization, Perry Huang was the straight line from New York to the Niger bridge.

Perry Huang was born in China, but schooled in design at the Ecole de Travaux Publique in Paris. He was modern in every sense and on a personal level towering in body structure—Perry was charming. The sand was running low on this Niger River Bridge Project which means the heads are rolling. It's get it done or die, of course, not literally.

Perry invited me to sit on the sofa across from his desk, which overlooked on one side Fifth Avenue, and began to brief me: "The hydraulic data upon which the bridge elevations were based are no longer valid. Niger is a young river, 2000 years old, and has not stabilized itself. Lake Debo in Mali is a large lake basin into which 12,000 M3 per second flow at high water. Lake Debo acts as reservoir and retains most of the flow. As a result only 2,400 M3 per second flow past Niamey at high water stage. However, the natural channels within the lake have changed since 1962, resulting in greater outflow. An increase of outflow of 1,000 M3 per second is enough to raise the level of Niger at Niamey 2 meters. Niger at Niamey has crested at elevation 180.51. However, the natural excavation of channels within the lake basin may result in an additional discharge in subsequent years." Pointing to a set of drawings of the bridge Perry continued "Abutment #3 was raised by changing the grade from Abutment #1 to the PVI, the vertical intersection of the curve for that bridge section. This is for you to ascertain."

He continued, "then there is the time factor. The XII Anniversary of proclamation of the Republic of Niger and President Diori's re-election. This means that the bridge must be open for traffic by December 18, 1970."

"As an additional factor there is halfway to the Libyan border, at Arlit, the strategic and immense uranium deposit, which everybody wants."

Perry now very carefully gave me two sets of the bridge specifications, one in English and the other in French as well as the set of the bridge plans we were looking at and suitably shook my hand saying, "Remo—good luck!" I smiled in return and said "Merci, A Toute a' l'heure", which is a French "I'll see you soon, I'll be in touch."

I collected the goods and with all of this well absorbed in my mind I left Perry's office. I was near the twin elevators when Perry came out calling "Remo, you have forgotten this" and he hands me the letters of introduction and credentials addressed to le Ministre des Travaux Publique of Niger, the telephone directory of the American Embassy in Niamey and the airline tickets.

I exited the building and parked in front was the small limousine that was to drive me to Kennedy airport. A young woman greeted me saying, "I am your driver, let me help you," and led me into the car. I directed her to go first to 5 east 67 street, at my floor-through apartment to pick up my suitcase and from there to Kennedy. The driver very efficiently answered, "yes sir!" and drove off. Later, leaving my place for the airport, I could not help noticing we were passing the 107th Regiment Memorial Monument at 67 St. and Fifth for which I laid out the new foundation some time ago when the Monument was moved from 65th and Fifth to give access to a transverse from the East to the West side. Further down as we drove on Fifth, the Corning Glass building came into view on 56th street and made me remember when I was the field engineer for the rock

excavation and foundation for that building for a Bronx excavation contractor, "Civetta," and "Fuller Construction," the construction manager.
On that site a crane with its boom horizontally at 0 degrees turned over,
going down on the iced wooden ramp. Luckily, no one was injured.

Then, as we passed 39th St. and 2nd I remembered the recording studio
of Columbia Records where I recorded an album of love songs for Columbia
entitled "Just Say I Love Her" by Remo Capra (now Romantic Standards).
It is a great album about which everyone, including the media, raved. It was
arranged and conducted by the well known composer and conductor Frank
De Vol and his string orchestra.

How that happened is still to me today a magic coincidence. I always
loved to sing, since it relaxes me and makes me feel happy, but I never
thought to do it professionally.

Here's how it happened. One day in New York, at one of the rock exca-
vations I was supervising, Gabe Pressman, the well known newscaster,
came to that job with his TV crew to record on film for the evening news
the rock blasting in NY and how it was done. He was sent to me for more
information and I explained to him in detail how we break rock in
Manhattan by sequential blasting. After that he asked me if I could sing
for him a few lines of a song, "Since," he said "as an Italian you surely
must know how to sing." I told him I'd be glad to and I sang for him a
few lines of a french song which I like "Vous Qui Passe Sans Me Voir"
which means in english "You Who Passes By Without Seeing Me." Gabe
Pressman thanked me and told me to watch the six o'clock news that
evening. I did, and was surprised to see myself on the news, singing on tel-
evision with my hard hat on.

After a few days, the former manager of orchestra leader Tommy
Dorsey, Tino Barzie, contacted me saying that Columbia Records would
like to give me a recording contract and would I like to meet Goddard
Lieberson, the president of the company. I said yes and after that meeting
I signed a contract with Columbia to record an album of popular songs.

Soon after, Dick Auletta, who was in the public relations field in New York, contacted me and invited me to appear on various TV Shows, such as, "What's My Line," "The Merv Griffin Show," "The Joe Franklin Show," and many others.

I could go throughout New York and pick up pieces of my past, but then I thought I should concentrate on my new venture and get ready for the upcoming unknown as we continued driving to JFK through the Midtown Tunnel.

As I sat now and relaxed in the back seat of the car, I began looking at the airline tickets and discovered surprisingly that my route has been changed. I was to leave for Niger from JFK at 8:00 PM on flight 700, TWA arriving in London the next morning at 7:35 AM.

Incident in London

We had done a half-spoon (a twisted 8) figure in take off over Kennedy. Like a white gauze, the slow clouds disappeared from view on our way to the altitude 35,000 feet. On a cuff count, as they would say in Monaco, that land of casinos, there is a full cabin tonight. Eleven in total. Yet the first class cabin was strangely empty in feeling almost like sitting in your den alone after having had friends over for the weekend for a good time.

Sandra the stewardess, was serving my scotch now, which she referred to as my "beverage." "Please note," Sandra says, "the two small pink malaria antidotes lying on the tray." I assured Sandra that I had taken all my vaccinations and even showed her my yellow card signed and stamped showing the malaria inoculation.

I was glued into my chair with the straps doubled over at the hinge. I began to cover the bridge specifications like a mystery book. Even to the unlearned, a set of specifications is a kind of intrigue. The general provisions of the contract, the strict enforcement of the specifications, the authority of the engineer, the time of completion, the penalties, the disputes.

I was settled back in my chair now, waiting for Sandra to bring my dinner, nursing my second scotch, and there was something that would not leave my mind.

Shortly before I left, a couple of evenings before to be exact, I left my apartment in the east sixties to go for a bite at Dick Edward, a local bar–restaurant.

That night, at the round table, where the locals always sit, was a scrawny thin railed tall man, with a black silk casino jacket and most remarkable hands. He greeted me and took me to my favorite seat. I always sat at the rear table by the round banquette table on the right. He gave me a menu, one for those on the "inside," and I order "steak well done; baked potato; and a full scotch."

I finished my drink when my neighbor, as he called himself, the man sitting next to me, says "I want to buy you a drink." Somehow he looked familiar to me. I looked over and said "I'm agreeable." Before I know it, the manager moves the old guy's silverware and plates to my table. It's very interesting how his dinner-ware is set. In fact he sets his own. He keeps a small black leather strip under his soup plate from which he eats his salad.

He didn't mince words. I mentioned "I am preparing for an oversea trip." He said; "I know where you are going. " Then he pulled several maps out of his jacket pocket and like a set gambler, showed me points of interest on the map. Interestingly, one of the maps was childishly done but very accurately portrayed: all the dock-ports of Africa and the cities were written in a very italicized handwriting. This map is signed; "I love you daddy."

I couldn't forget that night, and kept wondering how did this man know where I was going. Could he have been sent by Dr.ELP's office?

I doze in and out as we flew full with the northwinds. I would be in London in less than 7 hours. I've asked Sandra to wake me two hours before arrival. At that time, I dry-shave in the w.c. Back in my seat, I continued reading the bridge specifications. A bridge project was not a time to make new friends. I intended to relax until we landed.

May 15. We finally landed in London at Heathrow and, after the usual international arrival procedure, I jumped into a taxi and told the driver to take me to the Ritz Hotel. Soon after checking in at the Ritz, I asked the driver to take me to Chelsea Manor St. where my sister lived and to give her a pleasant surprise. Then I remembered that Christina, the sister of a friend of mine, Richie Berlin, was in London and decided to call her and chat a little. She answered the phone and was surprised that I was in London. We chatted a little reminiscing about the time when I was a guest at her parents' home in Rye, New York, with Richie and Richard her brother and the great time we had. Christina wished me good luck in Africa and I asked her to tell Richie that I am going to Niger.

But my short overnight stay in London did not go smoothly. A familiar face kept appearing now and then which made me aware that someone was following me. So I decided to go to a casino in the Knightsbridge section of London and have some fun playing roulette and to see if the familiar face would appear again.

Roulette has been a challenging game throughout the centuries and especially intriguing for kings and men of wealth and power. How well it is known in Monte Carlo. How many have jumped from a window or shot themselves for having lost their fortune to that invincible roulette wheel.

But I know that wheel well. 36 numbers divided into two colors. 18 numbers black and 18 numbers red. In the red color: 10 red odds and 8 red even. In the black color: 10 black even and 8 black odds. I once thought that by eliminating one of the two colors I would have an advantage of 10 versus 8 within each color. And so, I followed the voice of the croupier exclaiming "Rien ne va plus, Mesdames et Messieurs, rien ne va plus" and I got to that table and begin playing. When the red color would come I would follow the Red by placing the bet on the "Odds" on the carpet side of the table, and on the "Even" when the black color would come. So I played for awhile in that fashion, following a steady sequence of either color, but when the sequence would change alternating to Black-Red-Black-Red-Black, I would stop playing and wait for that sequence to change. I was winning quite a bit; being carefully assessed by the croupier and other casino officers. At one point, the zero showed up, I lost half of that bet and decided to quit.

I did not see that familiar face throughout my playing, not until I decided to walk back to the Ritz. As I was walking two men came out of a car towards me and one of them looking straight at me says "I want to talk to you". I knew at that very moment that it was not a time for hesitation and quickly turned back to the casino and went into the men's room to dispense with this unfriendly encounter. But soon enough, there they were behind me. Suddenly, like a flash, the familiar face appeared placing himself between me and the two men and with a speed I have never seen, he threw a round-house kick to the man in front of him, and a jumping-back kick to the one in the rear, knocking them out flat in an instant. Then, on the side, looking at me smiling, he says "I love you daddy" and left the same way he came. I knew then that he was my backup and an expert in Korean Martial Art (Taekwondo) because of the kicks he threw. I am a black belt in Taekwondo and recognized those kicks. I went back to my room at the Ritz Hotel, took all precautions and remained there until I was ready to leave the next morning for the airport to continue my journey to Niamey, knowing that the familiar face was there, somewhere.

Niamey

Neither the International British Airline nor TWA, I understand to this day, flies to West Africa, so that morning of the 16th I left London from Gatwick Airport on a one hour direct flight on Air France to Paris. Later on, Air Afrique would take me from Paris to Niamey. We landed in Paris at 12:25 PM and after the arrival procedure I signaled to a taxi, and I asked the driver to take me to the Champs-Elysee, to the GeorgeV Hotel. He stopped before the entrance on avenue George V and I hopped out. I walked straight to the main desk and I signed in. I intended to look around the hotel before I went to my room. After all, this luxurious hotel par excellence is named after George V, King of England, son of Edward VII. I might even run here into Greta Garbo who was known to be a regular at George V. But I am going into the hotel with the attitude "there is not a damn person here who knows me." and walked out the same way. In the evening, I decided to have dinner at the hotel restaurant and taste one of the french specialities "snails", although I was intrigued to order another intriguing dish, "lobster coated in chocolate sauce." The George V restaurant is well known to be able to serve its guests any dish they desire. The evening went by quickly.

The next morning, I thought of a friend, a poet who lived in Paris, Joanne Hart, at 13 Quai aux Fleurs on Ile de la Cite and I went to see her. She was glad to see me and we spent the day together reminiscing about New York and the time we spent in Princeton visiting an old friend of mine, Erich Kahler, at his home. Erich was a friend of Albert Einstein and a professor at Princeton University. He had written several books including "Man the Measure", "The Tower And the Abyss" and "The Rallying Idea."

In 1969 Joanne was in New York visiting from Paris and staying with a friend in the East 80's. When I saw her she asked me if she could meet Erich Kahler, knowing that I knew him. She had read some of his books and she would like so much to ask him about his writings and also about Albert Einstein. I said that I would try, not being sure, since Erich at that time was working on the writings of Thomas Mann and also translating some of Albert Einstein's letters. I decided then to do it, to bring Joanne to Erich's home and introduce her to him and chat for a few minutes. And so, on Sunday, January 10, we left New York in the morning and drove to Princeton. On our way we saw a farm food stand which had apples from a local orchard and bought some to bring to Erich. Before arriving I suggested that when we meet Erich not to talk but to mostly listen to him, he being one of the great minds of the world. "Joanne", I said, "if I begin to talk you kick me and if you begin to talk I'll kick you." Joanne agreed.

We arrived in Princeton and went directly to Erich's home at One Evelyn Place. Erich came to the door and was surprised to see me as I did not tell him I was coming. I asked Erich to excuse me if I just dropped in but it was just one of those things. Erich, as always, being most gracious, welcomed me and asked me who my charming friend was. I said her name was Joanne Hart, visiting from Paris, and a poet in need of some advice about her poetry. Erich asked us to come in but only for a few minutes since he had a deadline to meet. But then, our visit lasted two hours. We went into his library and Joanne was spellbound to see so many books all around the room stacked on the walls and on the table. There was a chair where Albert Einstein used to sit and Joanne asked if she could sit there. Erich let her and also read some of her poetry. Joanne asked if she should have it published and Erich replied "did you write it for your self ?" Joanne said "no." Erich then said that unless it was published it would not exist. He then invited us to go into the kitchen and have some tea and toast with anchovy butter to which Joanne said "isn't anchovy butter your brain food ?"That made Erich laugh. His answers to Joanne's questions were brief and with well chosen words. He gave her one of his books and he wrote in it "concentrate on the other person and then listen, listen, listen" and he signed it. It was an unforgettable afternoon with Erich Kahler which left Joanne spell-bound even to today.

I had a lovely time with Joanne that day in Paris, but soon, as always, time runs short and I had to say goodbye to my dear friend since my final flight to Niamey was at 8:15PM on Air Afrique. On May 18, 2:40 AM, I arrived in Niamey, Niger "River Among Rivers" in the language of the Tuareg people who dominate the north part of Niger.

I had never been in Africa and immediately I felt the change in climate. It was hot and dry. Once, someone told me that the French Legionnaires were sent here for disciplinary measures. At Niamey the temperature ranges from 47 F and 114 F. The arrival procedure with the Nigerien police before entering Niamey went smoothly: passport, visa, verifications, etc. As I exited the Airport I heard someone calling "Mr. Blois over here." It was the Pavlo representative who had been notified of my arrival and who came to pick me up. He had an open shirt and a gold chain around his neck going down his chest. He was robust and he looked very strong. He could have been a Marine at one time. "Hi, I am Harry Hand, I'm glad you made it. Please let me help you with your suitcase. We have an old Peugeot provided to us by the French contractor, as per our contract. It's an old car but it's OK. How was your flight? Any problems?" "Everything was fine" I said. "Surely it's hot here" I added. We entered the car and Harry began to drive.

I have been in many parts of the world but never did I have such strange feelings as I was experiencing here. Along the road you could see in the distance the light of oil lamps set up by traders. A heavy red dust in the air made the light which was emitted from the lamps, oscillate, looking red. Although strange, it was fascinating. The very old was now very present.

"I'm anxious to go through the files and all the logs (daily report) of the work since Klimof," I said to Harry "I understand there have been a few problems." Harry, smiling, replied "More than a few problems, no one gets along on this job. There is discord and misunderstanding among the contractors and Les Travaux Publique. And Klimoff, he was a good PE (Professional Engineer) but Africa was hard on him. Before he left, in his last days he began to see communists everywhere, even under his bed. He probably must be glad to be back home, in the USA. But for now, let me take you to the hotel where you are staying for the night and have a good rest. First thing in the morning, I will pick you up and we'll go to the bridge." "It sounds fine with me" I said. "I certainly need a rest."

After driving a while, Harry drove into an open area on the side of the road. There were huts spread apart in a circle with one in the middle which could have been the office where you sign in, although I did not sign in since Harry took me straight to the hut where I was to stay. "This is the hotel" Harry said. "You'll find it very comfortable. They have air conditioning in every hut." That's a relief, I replied. "I'll be able to study the plans and specs for awhile before I go to bed. I'll see you in the morning and thanks." "Pas de quoi, and sleep well" Harry said and drove off.

In a way, staying in an African hut seemed interesting, since I had never stayed in a hut before. The furniture was definitely African, with chairs and tables supported by elephant tusks, rugs made of tiger skin and shields and lances hanging on the walls. So I settled down, I assessed the bed under and between the sheets, in case there would be a spider or other poisonous insects or animals. I opened the french bottle of water that the hotel provided and only in my shorts I began studying the plans and the specs of the bridge. The remainder of the night passed quickly, although I woke up a few times. I definitely was excited and at the same time nervous to be on my first day's mission.

In the morning, punctually, Harry Hand knocked at my door and I was ready for him. I took all my things and entered the car. "Good morning

Remo." Harry said "Are you ready?" "Like an airplane" I replied, and so we took off on our way to the bridge.

We entered Niamey and drove on Rue Salaman, the main boulevard in Niamey named after a French captain. In the 1900's Niger became a French Colony until 1960 when it became independent.

But French administration continued to be as before the independence. In the commercial sector many enterprises belonged to French companies, such as the Bank of Paris, SOMAIR and other small companies. SOMAIR was connected with the French Atomic Energy Agency "COGEMA" for the exploitation of the large deposit of uranium at Arlit, in the Air Mountains. Niger had less than 20% in SOMAIR, but later it was raised to 30%. Eventually, the Government of Niger established their own mining corporation "ONAREM' which gave access also to other countries for the production of Uranium, including the international Spanish and Japanese "KOMINAC."

History shows that in Niger, before independence there were two political parties with completely different ideas how Niger should be socially structured. The "PPN" (Parti Progressiste Nigerienne) of Hamani Diori who favored association with France, and the left wing "UND" (Union Nigerienne Democratiques) also known as the "Sawaba" party, which did not favor the association with France.

Then in 1958 there was a referendum backed by Generale Charles De Gaulle and even though the Sawaba showed political strength, Diori came forth as the leader favored by France which supported him financially and militarily.

But, even though Sawaba was banned and it's leader, Djibo Bakary sent into exile Niger was covered by dissent. There continued to be plots against the government, guerrilla actions and acts of terrorism, including an attempt to Diori's life.

There was severe repression, and in Niamey seven people of Sawaba were publicly executed, being held responsible for those acts.

In the following years, Diori became involved also in International Politics. He mediated in the problem of Chad in 1968 and of Nigeria in 1967 both, bordering nations of Niger. He developed close relations with Canada and in 1967 he was invited by President Johnson to the White House. There, he reviewed the Guards of Honor with the President and thereafter he traveled extensively throughout the US studying our agriculture and the breeding of our cattle. In New York he visited the United Nations and there he gave a speech before the General Assembly.

"But, now" I thought "I wonder, what Diori's opposition will think of my arrival."

Soon we arrived at the bridge, at the left channel, according to the plans. The water of the river on the river bank was brown and there were women and men bathing and washing their clothes, and children splashing water all over trying to escape the very hot heat of the desert. I came out of the car and stood there looking at the bridge. Although not completed I could see and feel Perry Huang's design. It had a touch of Chinese. All the concrete piles supporting the piers had been driven, including the protection piles which are to stop or slow down any oncoming heavy debris that could hit and damage the bridge. I asked Harry Hand where is the field office and he pointed to the other side of the bridge at the end of the right Channel. " Follow me" Harry said and we began crossing the bridge walking on the beams, each 26 meters long, covering each span (21 in total) plus approximately 558 feet on land which is a small island in the middle of the river separating the bridge in two sections defined as the left channel and the right channel. I asked Harry Hand if there were any crocodiles in the river and he said "sometimes there are".

We arrived at the field office, a small square house with walls made of concrete with its roof of wood covered with tar paper, extending about 4 feet over the outside walls on each side. I walked around it to inspect the surroundings since I would spend most of my time here, directing the various operations, enforce the specifications, do the daily reports, estimates, computations, etc. While walking around the house I noticed in the back a large circle with piles of stones defining the circumference. I asked Harry what was the function of that circle and he explained that the guards guarding the office are Muslim and they use the area inside the circle each time they pray. They consider that area as being Holy Ground. I smiled thinking from the positive side that I too was blessed with a Holy Ground in the back of my office. We entered the office. There was a fan to cool off the room from the intense heat, a desk with an old dial phone, a file cabinet, a rack with plans and a table with a few chairs. Harry invited me to sit at the desk, since it was the resident's desk, and he sat down at the table. I asked him to show me the listing of the contents of the filing cabinet and he did. I looked at the plans in the rack and the most recent revisions and the specifications for the bridge that were there. We discussed correspondence between our people and the government of Niger and the American Embassy, the last estimate and the last payment made to the American contractor, the people involved and the positive and the negative of the operation.

Then I asked Harry if there was a small boat or a canoe that could take me to the river underneath the bridge to inspect the piles, the piers and the beams. "Yes! We have a small boat which belongs to the french sub-contractor" Harry said "we can use it any time we want." "Fine, let's see if we can have it now" I answered. Harry makes a telephone call to the french sub-contractor and within a half hour a man speaking french came to the office and said "Messieurs, le bateau est pret." We walked down to the river bank and entered the boat. It was a small canoe but it would do the job.

It took about three hours to inspect all the spans. The current in the right channel was quite strong and as we had to paddle against the current we moved slowly. I checked the clearance of the beams at the four middle spans of the bridge at the right channel and it was OK. At that point, the required clearance of the beams had to be no less than 6.05 meters from the highest water level. By now, Harry and I were exhausted by the heat and decided to

go to his residence, since between 12 and 3 in the afternoon the operation
on the bridge is shut down because of the high temperature.

Harry's home, which was provided under contract by the government
of Niger, was a big house. It had an open patio with lateral walkways
which had doors to various rooms at each side. There was a large kitchen,
bathrooms and showers. "The house provided to us is for free" Harry said.
"But, we have to pay for the electricity and the water which in Niamey is
very expensive." "Antoine, meet Mr. Blois, le nouveau patron" Harry said
to the house-boy who greeted us. He was a young Nigerien in his twen-
ties. He did the cleaning, laundry, the house chores and the cooking. He
was very efficient. "All your things are already here. I told Bawa, our
chauffeur to bring them here." Bawa was also a Nigerien, in his thirties.
"Well Mr. Blois I know you must be tired on your first day and want to
rest. I, for my part am leaving tomorrow and I have a few more things to
do before I depart and so, I will retire. I wish you all the best of luck and
success on your job. It was a pleasure meeting you." After having said this,
Harry shook my hand and went to one of his rooms. I have never heard
from him nor seen him since.

The Bridge

I was now settled in one of the rooms of the house provided by the government of Niger and I was feeling a sense of quietness. It was a large room with a screened window above the bed showing leaves from high plants outside. There was a shower and a bed rising high from the floor. The bed was already made and so I decided to take a shower and rest a little before dinner, but I overslept and woke at 5 AM.

Antoine, the house-boy, was already in the kitchen and I could smell the coffee he was making, so I dressed and began to inspect my new surroundings. "Bonjour Monsieur le Patron, vous avez dormi bien, j'espere. Voulez vous du café?" "bien sur", I said to the young man who was making sure that everything was to my satisfaction. I asked him what time Bawa comes in the morning, and he said, "usually at 6AM." I had the coffee and buttered toast that Antoine made for me and I began to get ready for my first day on the job. Bawa arrived, so I told him to take me to the bridge and to drive slowly so I could see my new environment.

Early in the morning it's cool and I could smell the vegetation along the way. On the road, we passed, slowmoving donkeys loaded with bundles of twigs and other farm animals guided by local men. There were shanty homes and people engaged in various activities and diverse crafts. One immediately knew that there was low economy and high poverty among the people in general. We arrived at the bridge at abutment 1, at the left channel, and I told Bawa to stay there should I need him later.

I began crossing the bridge spans and some of the workers who were already there greeted me with "bonjour, monsieur le chef, bonjour". They observed me with curiosity, almost like saying "how will the work proceed now, and what will you be like." I arrived at the office, greeted the guards and began to organize my things on the desk. Here I am I said to myself, with no one to ask questions, no one to give me advice and with a mission to accomplish so many miles away from the US. And so I began to review the field records, existing correspondence from the government of Niger and the contractors and various charts showing the progress of the bridge construction. I decided then to inspect the beams for the bridge superstructure and the bridge deck already poured with concrete. Of the 105 beams in total to cover all the spans, 101 were set in place. The remaining four beams, I thought, must be at the plant where the beams are cast. The plant was about 100 meters from the abutment on the right channel so I went to check it out. The area for the casting and post-tensioning of the beams and for storage material was laid out according to plans and the four beams were there in the curing stage, covered by a plastic-type sheet conforming to specifications. The bottom of the forms were placed on solid ground and I did not see any sag under the weight of the fresh concrete. I told the foremen in charge to make sure that if the forms and the waterproof membrane are removed from the beams before the seven days required for curing after the casting of the concrete, the concrete must be sprayed directly with water until the seven days curing period has elapsed. However, the bottom forms must be kept under the beams until the beams have been post-tensioned and are ready for displacement. The foreman assured me that he would.

(The post-tensioning of the beam begins with a starting load applied to each tendon for the purpose of taking up the slack in the tendon so that elongation measurements may be made when final tension is performed. This load is applied by hydraulic jacks and measured by jack gauges.

After the initial tensioning force has been applied to the tendon, reference points for measuring the elongation, due to additional tensioning force, are established. Thus, the stress induced in the tendon is measured by the elongation of the tendon and by the gauges. Post tensioning may be applied either from one end or both ends of the tendon. When the force is applied from both ends the force is applied simultaneously by jacks installed at both ends and must have the same magnitude at the same time.)

Back at the office the phone rang. "Good morning Mr. Blois, this is Gallinari, the vice-president of Brezina construction, the general contractor. Any information I can give you to help you get acquainted with the job?" I thanked him and replied that perhaps in a few days I would like to have a meeting of the minds in my office, including the french sub-contractor, and the GON. He assured me that he would notify the people concerned as soon as I decide.

It was now time for me to give my credentials to the GON and, later to introduce myself to the American Ambassador. So I went back to abutment 1 to the car and Bawa was there waiting. I told him to drive me to the Ministre of Travaux Publique since my letter was addressed to Minister Kaziende. With the letter in my hand I was escorted into the building to the office of the Ministre. A French man in civilian clothes was sitting at a desk before the entrance of the office with a revolver in an open holster strapped on his shoulder. I showed him the letter and he asked me to wait. After a minute or so he returned and made a gesture to me to come forward. He opened the door of the office and standing before me was Mr. Kaziende. He was very tall and congenial. He greeted me and I said "Monsieur Le Ministre, I bring you greetings from Doctor Pavlo, who has given me this letter of introduction addressed to you". Ministre Kaziende invited me to sit across from his desk and he began to explain the importance in finishing the bridge on time. "Already two extensions of time have been granted. The bridge was to be opened for traffic on April 21st 1970. An extension of 120 days was granted making the deadline to August 21st 1970. Considering all the work that still has to be done, it will not happen. It will be your main objective Mr. Blois to see that the bridge will be open for traffic by December 18, 1970." "Monsieur le Ministre," I replied "with your help and cooperation of all the people concerned I am confident that we will succeed." The minister thanked me and said should I need anything at all to call on him immediately.

I now directed Bawa to go to the American Embassy. He said that the new embassy building was still being built and he will take me to the old office. I entered the American Grounds and announced myself to the man in charge at the desk. I was told that the new Ambassador had not arrived yet, and that I was to see the Vice Consul, who came out and greeted me: "Hello, I am Stanley Escudero, the Vice Consul, please come in. We have been expecting you. Ambassador McClelland will be arriving in a week or so and he will want to meet with you. We are all hoping that everything will go smoothly from now on and that the Bridge will open on time." He assured me of his cooperation and that of his staff. I thank him and leave reassuring myself that so far everything looked good.

Returning to the bridge, I decided to drive, although Bawa thought it was not a good idea. "Patron," Bawa said, "there are too many animals roaming on the road and also kids. An accident would make the people very angry and they could turn on us. It would not be safe", I agreed with Bawa and so I let him drive, until I was more familiar with the streets in Niamey.

Back at the office, I entered in the log all the events of the day, wrote the daily report and decided to have dinner at one of the hotels in town. I called Antoine, the house boy, and told him that I would have dinner out and that he could have the evening off. I told Bawa to drive me to the hotel "Le Sahel", (the most chic hotel in town I was told) and that he could go to his home, have dinner and come back later.

At the "Sahel" there was a bar with seats at the wall along which people were sitting and drinking. I passed by the bar quickly and entered the dining room. It was a pleasant room on a terrace with a balcony, and one could see the grounds below with palm trees and plants. At one side of the room, there was a selected area for an oven and a marble bench to make pizza. I could see the young cook flopping the pizza into the air with agility and he was quite talented in his endeavor. His name was also "Antonio," brought in from Naples, Italy, for that purpose.

There were reserved tables for the usual customers, so I introduced myself to the head-waiter who spoke english, and he already knew who I was. "In a small town the word gets out fast," he said. He selected my table near the balcony and asked me what I would like. "Scotch on ice," I said, "and for dinner I'll take your suggestion". "Very well Mr. Blois, I recommend, if you desire fish of the day, a delicious trout or if you would like to have meat, a tender scaloppine al limone or with wine sauce." I thought about it and said "I will have a small Pizza."

I was immersed in my thoughts, when I noticed that there were people at some tables. They did not look American, so I asked the head-waiter who they were and he said "They are Germans at that table, and at the one next to it they are Russians. We have all nationalities here, including Chinese consultants for planting rice and Italians drilling for water wells." "Quite impressive," I said. So, I looked over to those tables and there was immediately a reciprocal nodding of the heads.

The pizza arrived and Antonio did not let me down. The pizza was delicious with mozzarella on top, and almost as good as the ones they make in New York. I ordered a glass of wine and enjoyed the pizza. I saw Antonio looking at me signaling with his thumb up. I signaled in return expressing my delight in the pizza. After a while the head-waiter came and told me that Bawa had arrived, so I paid the bill and left the dining room with the feeling that every-one in that room was observing me.

I passed by the bar and it was empty. I said hello to the bartender and introduced myself. He was pleasant and witty but spoke very little English. I ordered a cognac "Courvoisier" and asked him in French if the same people came here all the time and he said "mais oui, monsieur."

I wished him good night and went to the car where Bawa was waiting patiently. I sat in the front seat of the car and Bawa drove me home. The lights of the house were lit and I had no difficulty finding my way. I bid good night to Bawa and after inspecting all the locks, I went to bed. For my first day I thought, it went smoothly.

A noise at the window woke me up. It was early in the morning and I could see the light getting brighter and brighter. While I was lying on my bed I looked up at the window and could see the head of an animal jumping up and down trying to reach one of the leaves of the plants right outside the window. I stood up on my bed and reaching the window I saw clearly a red goat.

Strange that it was there since these goats are particularly found at Maradi, a small town near the Nigerian frontier. I knew this because a friend of mine in New York prided himself in having a "red goat skin" from West Africa. The goat must belong to someone, I thought. I showered and began to dress with my mind on the bridge and what would follow.

Antoine was up already and making breakfast. I went to the kitchen and said good morning. "Voulez vous un omellette, patron" the house-boy asked. I said yes and asked if he knew of a red goat roaming around the house. He said that since he has been in this house he has never seen one. I finished my breakfast and Bawa was waiting so I left for my second day on the bridge. As the first day, when I arrived at the office, the guards were there and the fan was on. I sat down at my desk and began reading a narrative report of the work to-date by the contractor. An estimate of 83% of the total completion was done. 105 beams of 105 were cast. Beams launched 101 of 105. Piers completed 19 of 19. Abutments completed 1 of 4. Abutments partially completed 3 of 4. Deck slab poured 15 of 21. Embankment 95%. Sidewalks on the bridge 20%.

I now decided to make my field inspection on the deck and I noticed that the bolts for the support of the lamp-post were being welded to the reinforcing steel of the sidewalk structure. I immediately stopped that operation and instructed the contractor to place extra steel bars where the welding occurred and to avoid all future and unnecessary welding since it weakens the reinforcing steel.

As I continued with the framing for the sidewalk, the top bars of the steel reinforcing were also being heavily welded to the steel bars, projecting from the top of the beams. I allowed them to do only some light tacking and instructed them to place an extra continuous longitudinal bar were the welding occurred.

They were beginning to pour concrete on one of the spans of the bridge deck when I saw that all the bottoms of the forms were not clean. Loose papers, rags, and small pieces of steel wires were at the bottom of the forms. The pouring of the concrete was stopped and the bottoms of the forms of the bridge deck were cleaned. I told the contractor that after the pour, all exposed freshly poured concrete has to be covered by burlap blankets overlapped at their joints and has to be kept wet by periodical spraying with water until the curing period has elapsed. I also told the contractor to have more supervision on the job. I knew then that the entire operation on this bridge had to be closely watched. By now it was past 11AM and I decided to take a ride in town and assess my surroundings.

We drove around Niamey and Bawa was most informative. Along the way you could see posh villas at one side of the road and in contrast nearby old men tilling the earth with some ancient hand tools. Niamey seemed to be cosmopolitan and at the same time holding onto an African rural life. As we drove, I saw the Presidential Palace displaying the flag of Niger comprised of three horizontal bands, green, orange and white, with an orange sphere on the white band, like the sun. "Ca c'est la Presidence" Bawa said, "Diori's residence, our Chief, who soon will run for re-election" "Who will you vote for?" I asked, "for Diori, naturellemente" Bawa replied, with confidence. "He will be our Chief for the next five years! I know now that the bridge will be finished on time." "Thank you for your good wishes." I said.

Bawa then showed me where he lived and introduced me to his family and his friends, who were very hospitable and friendly.

Back at the bridge it was very hot and dry and the work on the site was shut down until about 3 pm, except for the spraying of water on the freshly poured concrete. Soon, next month in June, the rainy season would start and it would be cooler. With that thought of relief in mind I went back to the office and continued working on the "work progress chart" that I was making for the completion of the bridge by December 18. I decided then to call Lucien Gallinari, the VP of the general contractor Brezina, and establish a convenient time for our general meeting with all the people concerned. We set the time for Friday the 22nd at 10am in my office.

At the meeting the first to arrive was Brezina's Gallinari, followed by Savioux representing GON, then Monteil, director general of Regie General, the french sub-contractor and Corbet, the engineer at large for Regie General. Gallinari had with him a big german shepherd so, I asked what was his name and he said "Rin Tin Tin". He made me remember that when I was little I had a german shepherd I called "William." After the formal introductions the meeting began with me holding in my hands the bridge construction specifications and saying: "This bridge is an A.I.D. project and has to be completed according to our specifications and design. There can't be any other way. Remaining materials and supplies, in connection with the construction and completion of the bridge, shall still have their source and origin in the United States or Niger, and their components also shall not be from a country not included in A.I.D. Geographic Code 935, except in cases of emergency and after my OK. Furthermore, all material and supplies for the completion of this project shall be shipped on privately owned US Flag commercial vessels. The contractor, shall make certain that no shipments are made on vessels listed in the latest "List of Free World and Polish Flag Vessels Arriving in Cuba since January 1, 1963" and in the "List of Free World and Polish Flag Vessels Arriving in North Vietnam on or after January 25, 1966." Those vessels are ineligible to carry A.I.D. financed cargo from the US."

Then, pointing at the progress chart I made, and to the items and quantities remaining to be done to complete the bridge, I continued "there are 22 items remaining to be done and I am sure we all know which of the items take precedence. Item 19 for example, there are four beams still to be set on the piers cap. In item 20, concrete superstructure, which includes the electrical and telephone conduits to be embedded in the concrete deck including the plastic bridge scuppers, there are still 617 cubic meters of concrete to be poured to complete all the spans. In item 6 we have 1100 square meters of bituminous concrete pavement to place including the roadway in the middle island and we have only 7 months to do it. I hope my chart, showing the progression of the work for each of the coming months will help you organize the work according to schedule".

There was a moment of silence after which Monteil of Regie General replied: "As you know, payments for work already done have often been delayed. We hope that with your authority you will now expedite future payments for each monthly estimate of the work done. If this is possible we shall have no problem in following your schedule."

"Bien," I said "we'll work together and I will be in the field checking and help you establish control points in order to check the centerline of the bridge and roadway, and bench mark elevations needed to establish the final grade of the bridge deck and of the roadway pavement. Finally, I must insist that all labor personnel on this job, old or new, must have strict security clearance from our office. These are also my orders. The meeting ended without controversy, and I was reassured of full cooperation from all people concerned.

The next day, on Saturday, I spent most of the time concentrating on past records of the bridge: previous estimate payments, records on the test made on the concrete cylinders of the casted concrete beams which require a strength of 5000 PSI (pounds per square inch) and records of the concrete piles 1.00M and 1.27M in diameter driven to the refusal line. I was now familiar with all the aspects of this operation and somehow I knew that I would succeed in finishing the bridge on time. The only obstacle now would be a natural disaster or sabotage from the opposing forces.

In the evening I had been invited by "le Charge d'Affaires des Etats Unis d'Amerique" at 7:PM to an exhibition of a Moon Rock at the "Centre Culturel Americaine".

It was very interesting to see one of the moon rocks that astronauts Neil Armstrong, Edwin E. Aldin and Michael Collins brought back from the moon in Apollo 11. That was the time when the US was racing with Russia for the moon.

Beginning with Surveyor 1 in 1966 to Surveyor 7 in 1968, to determine the hardness and bearing strength of the moon's surface for a safe landing. Followed then by the historical landing of the Lunar Module and Apollo 11, on July 20 1969, when man set foot on the moon for the first time and planted there the Stars and Stripes.

After the exhibition, I decided to go to the bridge and assess the night security at the site. There were no guards and the bridge was very accessible which made me think how easy it would be to bring damage to the bridge without even being noticed. Near Abutment 1, on the left bank, I could hear a drum beat and I went there to look. A group of local men were sitting and singing native songs. As I get closer they greeted me and knew who I was. So I sat with them and enjoyed their native music. After a while I said "Bonsoir" and left for my residence.

On Sunday Antoine and Bawa have their day off, so today I was by myself. As I got up I looked at my bedroom window, as I do every morning, to see if the red goat had reappeared, but I did not see him. I decided then to relax and drive to the American Center. There, they had a small swimming pool so I took a swim and enjoyed the fresh air in their garden. In the afternoon I went to the bridge and spent some time there. There was no one around and I had the feeling that the bridge and I we were "one on one," beginning to know each other, really meeting for the first time. Later in the early evening I decided to have dinner at a restaurant in Niamey beside "Le Sahel", so I went to Hotel Terminus where many Europeans went. I ordered a scotch and a well done steak. I had two scotches and then the steak arrived. I tried to cut it but it was as hard as leather. The situation reminded me of one of Charlie Chaplin's movies, where he was stranded in the snow for days without food and had to eat what he could. So he cooked the sole of his shoe, served on a plate and began to cut it and eat it making believe it tasted good. That scene still makes me smile, but I gave up on the steak in front of me. So I had another scotch, paid the bill, returned to my residence, to get a good night's sleep.

It was Monday and I went to the bridge early to organize myself for the day's work. The phone rang and it was a call from the American Consulate. I was asked to go there as soon as I could. Bawa was back so he drove me there. The General Service Officer, Emil Morin, greeted me and said " the Ambassador is not here yet and the Vice Counsel is away on business for a few days. According to our protocol you are on the chain of command and obligated to represent the USA by displaying our flag on your car when driving". He then gave me two small flags; one was the "Stars and Stripes" and the other a blue flag with white stars around the bold eagle saying "Pluribus Unum". I replied that I would be honored to display our flags on my car, even though the car I have is a french peugeot. And so for the next few days I represented the USA and it was a good feeling. No diplomatic emergency occurred and when the Vice Counsel returned I removed the flags from the car although I wished they could have stayed.

The bridge was progressing according to schedule and soon it would be time for me to review and approve for payment the monthly estimate of the work done. I was checking the material invoices and discovered that only 30 gallons of "Pozzolith Retarder," a water reducing retarding admixture for concrete, remained on the job site. This is a very serious matter for all concrete operations would cease without the retarder. I immediately called the contractor who in turn called the french sub-contractor. I was told that the Pozzolith Retarder was ordered two months ago, but for some reason the shipment was not received. I told them that a delay of the concrete operation would not be allowed and that the contractor must at all cost have on the job in the next two days the necessary quantity of the retarder, even if it had to be flown directly from France. After a long search the Pozzolith was found, and fortunately I did not have to take extreme measures.

We were now in the rainy season and the sudden, but, short heavy rain in the middle of the day always brought a pleasant relief from the heat. I was in the office examining my mail and there was a small envelope from the American Embassy. It was an invitation to a reception at the new embassy building to greet the new Ambassador, Roswell D. Mc Clelland and his wife. It would be very interesting and helpful to meet him and I was anxious to hear what he had to say about the bridge. So, I went to my residence, cleaned up, put on a well pressed shirt and a conservative tie and told Bawa to drive me to the new embassy.

At the reception there was a large crowd, including other diplomats and representatives from the GON. I was introduced to the Ambassador and as I expected he asked me to please call him at the office to set up a meeting to discuss the bridge and its progress.

The next morning I called and in the afternoon went to the embassy. The construction of the embassy building was complete, although there were still some final details to be done. I was welcomed by a slim lady who said "I am Mary Lou Harvey, the Ambassador's secretary, the Ambassador is waiting for you," and graciously escorted me into the Ambassador's office. The Ambassador greeted me and asked me to sit down, saying " I've heard good things about you and I am glad you are here. As you know, there can be no other extension of time for the completion of the bridge and we are all relying on your skill, competence and dedication. Africa's destiny 'quote', is of direct concern to the United States. The desire of Africans to shape their own destiny continues to find the logical and material response in America. This bridge, which is an American bridge is a means of progress for the people of Niger and needed to develop the other side of Niamey with schools and other modern facilities for the advancement of their education. They need this bridge in order to remain free and independent."

After having listened attentively I replied, " Since the 18th of May, when I arrived, things on the bridge have gone smoothly. The American general contractor "Brezina" is represented by Lucian Gallinari and the French sub-contractor "Regie General" by Mr. Monteil. I've also met Minister Kaziende of the GON, including their engineering staff, and they all have assured me of their cooperation. After having assessed the past and present operation of the bridge, I did make a progress chart for the work to be done and which the contractor and sub-contractor must follow. But, because of the election of the incumbent President Diori, we might have some attempts to delay the completion of the bridge by the opposition. As we all know " Sawaba" and his left wing party, who are backed by other left wing countries including the "People Republic of China", opposes any association with France. Even though Sawaba has been banned and Bakary, the leader of the party, driven into exile, there could still be attempts by them to damage the operation. And then there is also the huge deposit of uranium at Arlit, half-way to the Lybian border, which is a great attraction. These are serious factors that could bring about another delay in the completion of the bridge by December 18,1970. As far as the work is concerned, I am making sure that everything is done according to specification. On the part of Washington AID, the monthly payments to the contractor for the work done for each period must be expedited and that is necessary, of course, only after I have given the OK for the quantities and the quality of the work done". Ambassador Mc Clelland, after having listened without interruption shook my hand and smiling at me said "We'll see what we can do".

John F. Kennedy Bridge
American Embassy, Niamey
Niger 1970

The Attempts

On the job today the men were ready to set the beams on the pier cap and the abutment. The beams will be rolled on a lorry on tracks to the closest and most convenient span. The beams will be transported in an upright position and points of support and direction of reaction with respect to the beams shall be approximately the same during transportation as when the beam is in its final position. Extreme care will be taken in lifting or lowering the beams to prevent cracking due to excessive stresses or impact. We will also begin working on the Island Roadway which connects the bridge spans of the left channel to the bridge spans of the right channel. So the bridge operation was going according to schedule and there seemed to be no serious problem, except for the material with which to build the Island Roadway. Our design and specifications call for a base course of aggregate. However, the french sub-contractor and the GON insisted in making a change from aggregate to laterite, a material found in the region. I personally do not favor the laterite, but considering the economical factor and that it is a GON road to maintain, I have advised AID and the Ambassador that I have no objection.

And so, at a meeting at the GON which included Mr. Chidester and our newly arrived Sarah Jane Littlefield of U.S. AID, the French sub-contractor, the American contractor and several officials from Travaux Public, the change order to laterite was given and several other problems were also resolved. After the meeting I chatted for a little while with Sarah Jane and found her to be precise and efficient. We later went to her office in the new Embassy and it was impressive. A big desk with a big American flag behind and a front office where her secretary, Elaine Crooke, did her typing and other work. We discussed the bridge at length and she reassured me of her help and cooperation and told me that I should keep her informed should any problems arise. I surmised that it would be a good working relation and that she would be of great help on the direct line to Washington.

Going back to the bridge on the Island Roadway the men were compacting the stripped soil surface. However, I noticed that there were several pockets of wet soil coming up to the surface. I insisted that they remove in depth those pockets before compacting the embankment again, upon which the aggregate course was to be placed. Now, of course, the laterite would be used instead.

After work, in the evening I decided to have dinner at Le Sahel. I stopped at the bar first, said hello to the bartender and had a scotch with ice. There was a big crowd, mostly Europeans and I joined a man with a white beard smoking a pipe who came to me and introduced himself as Dr…I asked where in Europe he came from and he said "Lugano, Switzerland". He was here in Niger doing medical research.

A little later an American came and asked me about the bridge. He was interested in the progress of the operation. He was from Texas working for a company called Global Energy. I asked what he did and he said that he was in aerial surveying of land strata, but that at the moment he was at a stand still. One of the two motors of his plane became inoperative and he was waiting now for a new one coming from the U.S. But, for some reason, the new motor has gotten lost somewhere in Abidjan. I wished him good luck and told him that something similar had happened to me, when the Pozzolith Retarder shipped from France could not be found, but that later did show up.

Back at my residence, I went to sleep thinking of all the things happening, and in reality, I expected much worse. In fact, so far, everything had gone so smoothly that I thought perhaps this was the calm before the storm. In the morning as I was waking up I heard a noise. I stood up on my bed and, looking out my window, I was surprised to see the red goat. I quickly put on my robe and rushed outside to the back of the house hoping to catch him, but when I got there he was gone. I asked Antoine if he had seen the red goat but Antoine said he did not. Was I beginning to have symptoms of paranoia as Klimoff had? Absolutely not, I told myself, my mind was strong and well trained. Most likely the red goat belongs to a neighbor who lets him loose in the early morning. Nevertheless, if he were to show up again, I intended to catch him and examine him closely.

Bawa did not appear for this morning, so I drove to the bridge. There was a message with the guard. Bawa was suffering from a hangover from the previous night. On the bridge, while doing my usual inspection, I noticed that a heavy steel barge about 60 feet long was anchored on the left bank, in the river upstream, in the direction of Abutment 1. I did not like the idea of that heavy barge being where it was. Should the barge get free from the anchor or the ropes that were holding it, it would definitely come down on the river and hit one of the pile columns supporting the bridge and cause serious damage. I brought it to the attention of the foreman of the job and he reassured me that he would make 100% sure that the barge would not get loose and that he would move it to a safer location. Nevertheless, I had a camera with me and took a picture of the barge.

After work I retired early and decided to spend the evening at home and relax. The heat of the day could really exhaust one. So I decided to skip dinner and have a cool French beer while reading a French novel. After awhile I fell asleep. In the middle of the night, again a noise woke me up. I always had a flashlight near my bed, should the electricity fail. So I jumped up to the window and pointed the flashlight in the direction of the noise and there it was, the head of the red goat looking straight at me. I quickly ran to the back of the house, but again he was gone and everything was normal again.

I went back to my bed and tried to sleep again when, suddenly the noise started again. This time I did not jump to the window, but instead, moving very silently, went to the back of the house to try and catch him by surprise. I had my revolver in one hand and the flash light in the other but when I flashed the light the only thing I saw were his hind legs hopping up and down as he made his escape.

By now it was close to 4 AM and there was no point in trying to go back to bed, so I put on some clothes and decided to drive to the bridge. When I got there the night guard, newly hired and approved by me, greeted me and asked if I needed assistance. I said thank you and that I only needed a walk on the bridge. I began walking when I heard something underneath the bridge hitting one of the pile-columns. I rushed down to the bank and there was the steel barge swinging from left to right hitting the pile columns. The barge had gotten loose from one of the ropes tied to the bank at Abutment 1. If this continued, without any question the pile-column would have been damaged. I called the guard thinking that perhaps the two of us could pull back the rope tied on the barge and stop the barge from swinging but we could not do it. The barge was too heavy. So I went to the office and called the emergency telephone number of the GON and asked for immediate help. Within 20 minutes a crew of men arrived and were able to immobilize the barge. While this went on a car arrived and it was Minister Kaziende. He came to me and greeted me shaking my hand wanting to know what had happened. I explained what the barge was doing and also posed the question why was the barge so close to the bridge. "The barge, Monsieur Le Ministre, should have been anchored on the other side of the bridge, that is, downstream" "Monsieur Blois" Minister Kaziende answered "the Government of Niger thanks you for your alertness."

This event reminds me of one of my favorite fables from Fedro, the Greek moralist. Fedro wrote "Lupus et Agnus at Rivam Venit. "That is" The wolf and the lamb came to the same river. The wolf was upstream and the lamb downstream. Now, the wolf who had already decided to make a meal of the lamb and trying to find an excuse, said to the lamb, "Little lamb, why are you making my water dirty?" The lamb answered, "Mr. wolf, how can I make your water dirty since you are upstream and I am downstream?" The wolf being defeated, and having no other excuse, replied "Then, your mother must have dirtied it at another time," and he ate the lamb.

So with everything back to normal I decided to go back to the house and have breakfast and pick up Bawa who by now, I was sure was waiting to resume his position. On my way back I thought, in retrospect, that if the red goat had not persisted in keeping me awake, in the morning we would have cause for a delay in the progress work schedule and in the date for the opening of the bridge to traffic. Next time I hear a noise at my window, I resolved, I would reward the red goat with some fresh plant leaves.

I was now back in my office on the bridge and I had to call for a meeting to investigate why the barge was relocated near Abutment 1 and why one of the ropes holding the barge got loose. Is this a case of negligence? Or was it intended? Was it a pure accident? Even so, the rope should not have become untied from the steel barrier set on the bank. So I called in the foreman of the job to meet with him one on one.

The foreman came within a short time and I asked him to please sit down. "As you know," I said, "early this morning one of the ropes holding the barge at bay became untied and the barge was swinging back and forth hitting one of the pile columns. First, the barge should have been relocated on the other side of the bridge, downstream, and second, why wasn't the one rope secured enough so this could not have happened?"

The foreman was upset and asked me to please listen to him and that what he did was in fact to try to make it safe so the barge would not hit the bridge. I said, "Go ahead." So, he replied, "Chef, because of the strong current in the river, I thought the barge being close to the bridge would have been safe. Even if by accident it had gotten loose, it would have stopped at the pier column without impact. I personally made sure that the ropes were securely tied to the steel barrier on the bank. I do not understand how the one rope became untied by itself".

I analyzed what he said and came to the conclusion that, although he was responsible for what happened, it was not ill-intended. So I told him to go back to work and to relocate the barge on the other side of the bridge or to get rid of it. But one thought stayed in my mind; "How did the one rope get untied?" from now on I have to be extra watchful on every step of the bridge operation.

In the evening, I was invited by Mr. Monteil of Regie General, to have dinner at his residence and later for an after dinner drink at the French club. I welcomed this invitation which would give me access to the French circle and become familiar with their life style.

The Attempts
(PART 2)

We were at the end of August and there were 16 Items left to complete the construction of the bridge. Except for the aggregate base course or the laterite and the bituminous concrete pavement to be placed on the roadway and two spans for the deck concrete slab, most of the items dealt with the lighting of the bridge, the steel guard rail, catch basins and concrete curbs. We had approximately four months to the deadline and, without interference, according to my schedule, we would make it.

On the roadway today I checked the compacted surface for the road sub-grade and its total width. I asked the foreman for his assistance which he efficiently gave me. I used an old French level instrument on a tripod, which the contractor had loaned me, to set a one foot mark above the required elevation on the wooden stakes driven into the ground by the foreman every 25 feet, on each side of the roadway. Then from a string line, which I tied level with the marks on the stakes, going across from both sides of the road, I measured the depth from the string to the compacted surface and found the sub-grade to be OK.

Back at my office I began preparing Estimate 20 for the work done in the month of August and which I would compare to the estimate that the contractor Brezina would most surely send me the next day or so for me to sign and for him to get paid.

The day went smoothly and in the evening I went to Le Sahel for one of Antonio's pizza and a cool beer and to see if there were new faces at the tables. The dining room was full, but the headwaiter always kept a table available for me, so he greeted me and led me to the table next to the terrace balcony. As I looked around I saw Sarah Jane Littlefield and her secretary Elaine Crooke at one of the tables. We waved at each other and after a while the headwaiter brought me a message from them "would I like to join them." I said yes and went to their table. They had already ordered their dinner and I told them that I was having a pizza made by Antonio, which I always found to be very tasty. Antonio again gave me the victory sign and I did the same. We chatted and gossiped a little about all the different nations which were represented in the dining room and laughed a little. After dinner I insisted that they be my guests and signaled to the headwaiter not to bring the check to the table. They graciously accepted and we said good night.

As with every night, I felt exhausted from the heat of the day and a cold shower always rejuvenated me. So I took a shower and before I went to sleep began rethinking the decisions I had made and the work that was done during the day. Then I wondered if the red goat would reappear in the morning and after a while I decided to go to sleep.

It was 5 AM, the usual time for me to wake up and there was a noise at the window. The red goat is back. At least he did not wake me up in the middle of the night, I said, and as I promised I would give him his reward. So I went to the kitchen and took some fresh plant leaves that Antoine had gotten for me and went back to the window. Then I opened the screen and tied the leaves to a string, lowering them below. I set back the screen the way it was and quietly tried to listen if the red goat would come for it, but there was complete silence. "I will check it later" I said, and went to the kitchen for breakfast. Antoine was making coffee and intrigued by my inquiries about the red goat asked me if I wanted him to try to catch him. I said not to worry and that the red goat is now a friend of mine. Bawa arrived, but before leaving for the bridge I went to the window in my room to see if the red goat had eaten the leaves and as a pleasant surprise the leaves were no longer there, which made me smile. The red goat had taken my reward.

On the way to the bridge, I began wondering if the reappearance of the red goat was not another sign or warning for something happening on the bridge. On the bridge I looked for the barge but it was no longer there. I checked all the beams and the pile-columns, including the pier caps. I had covered all the critical points except the end beams for expansion at the abutments. I well remember back home on the Narragansett Bay Bridge in Newport, Rhode Island, how once Jack Kinney, the Resident Engineer of that project, asked me not to forget to check the "rocker lean" under the beams, which were needed for the expansion movement of the beams at the Abutment, and to make sure that the rockers were set to the degree specified. So after arriving at the office and after having checked the mail, I went to check the beams at each Abutment and at Abutment 1 there was a problem. At the expansion end of the beams, the slotted holes of the bearing plate were not centered with the centerline of the anchor bolts on the Abutment, obstructing expansion and fixed as if they were at the fixed end beam.

I called Sarah Jane Littlefield and told her that I had to see her about a matter that could not be discussed on the phone. She can come to my office or I go to her office. It was decided that I would go to her office. I explained to her the function of the slotted holes of the beam bearing plate in relation to the centerline of the anchor bolts for expansion at the Abutment and that this is a very serious matter. I also said that unless this situation was corrected immediately and according to design, I would not sign the August work estimate done by the contractor and I would have to ask AID to hold all payment until this situation was resolved. Sarah Jane Littlefield agreed with me and said that she would refer the matter to her boss.

Back at my office I put in a call to Brezina's Lucien Gallinari and told him the same thing. Unless this problem is immediately corrected, no payment would be forwarded to the contractor or the sub-contractor.

The Attempts

(Part 3)

For the next few days there were discussions back and forth with the contractor and the French sub-contractor on how to correct the slotted holes at the expansion beam end, and also the safe and best way. I was now in my office and received a call from the "Union Nationale de Travailleurs du Niger", the only trade union in Niger with approximately 15,000 worker members. "Monsieur le Chef, in the afternoon our delegation will come to your office on the bridge to discuss with you why the wages of the workers for this week are not available and we want to find an immediate solution to this situation."

This took me by surprise. I called the contractor but there was no response. So I called the French sub-contractor and Monteil came to the phone. "Mr. Remo, we have no extra money in our funds to pay this week's wages to the workers. As you know, the payments for the work done in August have been stopped at the bank in New York. I have no other alternative but to send the workers to you for their week's pay". I did not answer. I knew I was in trouble. If I released the payments I had no guaranty that the problem at the expansion end beam would be corrected satisfactorily and if I didn't, the bridge would come to a standstill with a strike by the workers and the danger of some violence. A strike would also clearly create a delay and give an opportunity for the forces opposing Diori to take advantage of the situation and create dissent. I called Ambassador Mc Clelland and I asked if I could come to see him about an urgent matter. He said "yes" and so I immediately went to see him. "Mr. Ambassador", I said, "I need to borrow some cash so I can pay the workers their week's pay. The French say that they have no money because we've stopped their payments in New York, of money due to them. So they have referred the workers to the Americans for their pay. A delegation from the Trade Union of Niger is on its way this afternoon to my office on the bridge to discuss the matter. Could I borrow enough cash from the Embassy to pay for the workers wages?" The Ambassador rings his secretary to find out how much money there is in the Embassy's vault. Then smiling at me he says " I guess if we don't find the money they will hang you from a tree." I smiled in return and thanked him. I knew I had the money.

So back at my office, I reflected for a while and waited for the delegation to arrive. Finally, they arrived and I welcomed them. It was a delegation of twenty but one of them made the introductions and before the discussions could commence I calmly stated; "Dear friends by tomorrow the workers will be paid. If not by the French sub-contractor they will be paid by me. Please refer this to the workers. And for today, they will all have lunch on me". The delegation thanked me and spoke to the workers who were outside my office. They all cheered and went back to work. I then sent Bawa and the laborer foreman with the car to buy enough food for all the men.

The next morning I received a long distance call saying "The money is in Paris" and then there was a hang up. Strangely, the voice sounded familiar. I immediately called Monteil at Regie General and repeated the message "l'argent est a Paris." Monteil hearing this, said that he would check with his office in Paris and if the monies were there, then the problem was resolved. "Not so," I said. "You cannot pour the concrete slabs for the last two spans until you have centered the slotted holes of the beam bearing plate with the anchor bolts at the beam end expansion." Monteil guaranteed to me that it would be done. I said that I would be there to check it. We later found out that the money was in Paris and the workers were paid the same day.

It was a long day and an exhausting day, but at least the work on the bridge was back on schedule with a minimum delay. I am now anxious to see the problem of the beam end expansion resolved, but I had no other choice. I had to wait until tomorrow. If tomorrow there is no action, I said to myself, I will put pressure on Monteil through minister Kaziende.

I went to sleep and during the night the red goat awakened me several times, so I woke up late. The sun was bright but the air was cool. Bawa was waiting, so I had some coffee and went to the bridge. When I arrived at the office there was a message from Gallinari. To please call him. So I did, and on the telephone he told me that the problem of the beam expansion was resolved. The sub-contractor had worked all night and corrected it. I was upset by this since I wanted to be there when they did it. But, then I thought, it can't be true. How could they have done it so fast? I told Gallinari I would call him later. So I went to the Abutment and indeed the slotted holes of the bearing plate of the beam were centered with the centerline of the anchor bolts. I then wondered how they did it. I decided to ask the contractor to give me a detailed report on this operation. And so, after having inspected the beams for possible damages, and there being none, I gave the OK to pour the concrete slab for those two spans.

The Plaque

We were near the end of the job, all the items having been completed except for the installation of the electrical distribution panel. The concrete footing for the panel was already poured and the open ends of the conduits were all capped. I was satisfied with the progress of the bridge. I think we've made it!, I said to myself.

In the mail that day I received an invitation from Sarah Jane Littlefield to attend a reception at her residence on Sunday, the 25th of October, between 5PM and 7PM, in honor of Mr. Birbaum and Mr. Spencer of AID, Washington. "Chemise vest." So on Sunday I had the pleasure to meet Mr. Birbaum and Mr. Spencer, who were very amicable and interested in what I had to say. The reception was well organized and Sarah Jane a gracious host. There was a bar and a bartender who knew how to mix all kinds of drinks. I saw Gallinari chatting with the two guests and I wondered what they were saying. Later, Sarah Jane came and asked me if I would like to join her and the two guests and go for a drink in one of the clubs in Niamey. I said, "I'd be delighted".

The club was a discotheque with private booths along the side and we sat in one of them. I noticed that Gallinari had also joined us, which I did not mind. The music was amplified and mixed with American and French songs, having been given a disco beat. The rotating and flickering lights and the strong beat induced the people to dance. I enjoyed watching some nigerien girls and boys dancing to those beats and at one point I was tempted to do the same. But then I thought, I would have looked ridiculous not being able to swing in time with that beat, and so I remained seated to enjoy my scotch. While chatting with Birbaum and Spencer, as

I expected, they asked me about the bridge. Thus, I invited them to have a tour of the bridge, the next day if they liked. They responded that it was their original wish and that they were going to ask me exactly that. "Well" I said "I'll meet you then at the bridge tomorrow morning at 9AM if that's OK with you." They thanked me and we all decided to end the evening with a pleasant "au revoir" and "bonne nuit".

In the morning, at 9AM sharp, I met Birbaum and Spencer at the bridge. I noticed that they were dressed for the tour. They both wore a summer hats and loose shirts. I greeted them and began showing them the bridge by walking first to the right channel at Abutment 4. From there we walked toward the middle of the bridge and I explained to them the highest point at that spans in relation to the water level, the vertical curve of the bridge and the pre-stressed concrete beams. When we arrived at abutment 1, they asked me if they could see the slotted holes of the bearing plate at the expansion end of the beam and the anchor bolts. I told them that they would have to come underneath the beams on the Abutment, to see it. They said OK and we all went underneath. I explained to them that at the other end of the beam, the holes are round, and that is the fixed end of the beam. But at this end the holes are slotted and centered with the anchor bolts to allow expansion. They found my explanation interesting and again they thanked me and should I be in Washington to please give them a call.

And so at the end of October we were in good shape, especially since President Diori has been re-elected. We were now ready to set the project plaque. The plaque was made of stainless steel and was placed at the north end-post of Abutment 1 on the Niamey side and anchored in the concrete with 9 steel tap bolts of ¼ inch in diameter and 0,100 meter long. The lettering was engraved and filled with black color epoxy enamel and it read:

PONT JOHN F. KENNEDY
PROJET DE CONSTRUCTION ENTREPRIS
PAR

LA DIRECTION DES TRAVAUX PUBLICS ET DE L'URBANISME
DE
LA REPUBLIQUE DU NIGER
AVEC LA COLLABORATION DE
L'AGENCE POUR LE DEVELOPPEMENT INTERNATIONAL
AGISSANT POUR
LES ETAS UNIS D'AMERIQUE
1970
INGENIEUR CONSEIL: E. LIONEL PAVLO, NEW YORK,U.S.A.
ENTREPRENEUR: THE BREZINA CONSTRUCTION COMPANY, INC.

THE DRIVE

During the month of November most of the work involved paper work, final acceptance, calculating final quantities for payments to the contractor and other final details. So everything was going well and I was satisfied with the bridge. I now ventured with Bawa into the interior of the country whenever I could and enjoyed watching giraffes and other animals that roam the wild. I had also attended the local race track and watched a camel race run by Tuareg warriors, robed all in blue, looking majestic. It was an exciting experience watching the camels spurred by the Tuareg to a very fast pace. They made me think of "Timbuktu" that fascinating city in the Sahara desert which always brings an air of mystery when someone mentions it's magical name.

The Tuareg are one of the many tribes that comprise the population of Niger. For example; there are the Fulani people, the Hausa, the Songai-

Zerma, the Kamuri, the Buduma, the Sokaro, the Woko and Toubou. They all live in different ways and subsist by different means and they have their own language.

The Tuareg are a nomadic people and like the Fulani, they wander the desert with their live stock. The Tuareg travel with their goats, sheep and dromedairs, live on meat and dates and shelter themselves in tents while the Fulani, in addition to their live stock live mainly on milk products and have impermanent shelter. The Tuareg language "Tamashek", from which the name Niger, "River among Rivers," derives, is also spoken in nearby countries including Mali and Algeria. Agadez was their old capital and hosts today, still, desert caravans.

My office was now officially in the American Embassy. I was on the first level floor to the right as one entered the Embassy. Across from me was the doctor's office and clinic for the Embassy employees and American personnel. Mine was a small office but sufficient for what I had to do. The Ambassador's office was above on the second floor and so was the office of Sarah Jane Littlefield, whom I saw now almost every day, as I went over the final quantities and final payments to the contractor. I felt comfortable working in the Embassy although I missed being on the other side of the bridge, and the morning walk from Abutment 1 to Abutment 4.

Bawa was still my driver and I had become fond of him. He always gave me the news and gossip of what people said and thought of me. He always said that he was proud to work for me, but he knew that soon the bridge would be finished and I would have to leave and that made him sad. I told him that everything would be alright for him, since he spoke english and I would give him a letter of reference.

One evening I crossed the bridge in the car past Abutment 4, to go further into the interior and check the condition of the existing road. I told Bawa that I would drive tonight and that he should relax. So I turned the switch on, but the engine would not start. After a few times trying to start the car, I went outside to check what was wrong. The spark plugs were OK and so was the oil. There was no gasoline. I asked Bawa why was there no gas, but he reassured me that he had filled the tank fully in the afternoon. I checked the tank for a possible leak but there was none. "I swear, I said to Bawa, that if the red goat was a man, I would think without any doubt that this was a trick pulled by him". "Maybe it's his spirit" Bawa said. "I believe in spirits, Chief!" I replied, smiling, "It could be". Bawa went and came back with a can of gasoline, enough to drive to the garage of Regie General and refill our tank.

We drove for a while on the road going into the interior and the road was bumpy and dusty. From far off I could see the bright lights of an oncoming car. The lights were blinding me, so I decided to stop and let it go by. The oncoming car was going at a fast speed and raising heavy dust all around. When close to us a sudden cracking noise shook us up. I went outside and there were no signs of damage to the car. I went back inside and then I saw at my far left a ½" circular crack in the front window. Then I heard Bawa saying "Chief, there is a hole in front of the window where I am". We were both amazed at what had happened. Did the passing car take a shot at us? And if so, with what? Could two little pebbles from the road have sprung up from the tires of the oncoming car? Whatever it was, according to Bawa, Allah was with us. "Allah, Allah was with us, chief, Allah" Bawa kept saying throughout the entire drive back. In the morning, I personally drove the car to Regie General and asked them to change the glass in the front window. They also thought that it was a strange accident to happen.

The Bridge Ceremony

We where into November and the long dry season had begun and would last until June, while the winter rains ended with October. On the bridge all the railing had been erected including the light poles and the electric distribution panel. Except for the final load test to be done on the bridge, everything seemed to be ready for the bridge to be opened for traffic.

Meanwhile on November 5th, I was invited by Charles Meyer to a cocktail party and met there other officials from AID.

And on November 26th, I was invited by the General Service Officer of the American Embassy, Emil F. Morin and his wife to have Thanksgiving Dinner at their home. Emil played piano, so we had fun singing to his piano accompaniment.

On November 28th, I was invited by the Building Supervisor Officer, Bruce Smith, to a buffet dinner. I was delighted with these invitations which I did attend. I certainly needed the relaxation.

And so the month of November went by quickly, but now I had to decide where on the bridge, at which span, I would make the load test. After reflecting, I decided to do it on Span 13, which is on the right channel between Abutment 3 and Abutment 4. I asked the Ambassador if I could use the Embassy Diplomatic pouch for me to send some correspondence to Dr. Pavlo in New York and the Ambassador gave me the OK. So I sent my calculations for the load test to Perry Huang in New York for him to check it. After a few days, Perry called me by telephone and said "Remo, go ahead". I called then for a meeting with the contractor, the sub-contractor and the GON, to decide how to make the load test. It was decided to use trucks loaded with bags of cement. "For how long" they asked. I directed to let the load remain on the bridge span all night. And so it was done. The load test was a success.

In the early morning the trucks left the bridge and it was time for the beams inspection. I asked one of the GON representatives to go with me in a small boat underneath the bridge at Span 13 and the adjacent spans to check the beams. I verified that there were no cracks or any visible damages in the beams and returned to shore.

Back at my office I wrote an official note to minister Kaziende saying: "Monsieur le Ministre, I am happy to inform you that the bridge is now ready to be opened for traffic". I also advised the Ambassador and Sarah Jane.

Time seemed to go by slowly now. I guess it was because I was anxious to open the bridge for traffic on the 18th. But the invitation I had just received from Ambassador Mc Clelland, to attend a reception at the Embassy on December 17th to greet 3 previous American Ambassadors: Cook, Ryan and Adams, made it interesting to wait.

At the reception there was a line up of many dignitaries from the GON and other officials, who came to greet them, including Gallinari and Monteil. We all stood in line and one by one we shook hands with the three Ambassadors. It was an interesting reception and we all talked about the ceremony of the opening of the bridge to be held the next morning. Later in the evening, before retiring, I took one last ride by myself on the bridge and stayed there for awhile. I thought of President Kennedy having a bridge named after him in West Africa and of 1963 when the country was in mourning.

In the morning I put on a suit and a tie and drove to the bridge. There was lots of excitement. People were gathering on the bridge sidewalk waiting for President Diori to arrive. Ambassador Mc Clelland and his wife arrived and so did American Ambassador Ryan. With them was J. A. Abbott and his wife representing President Nixon. At 10AM the invited guests and Nigerien personalities began to arrive. They were followed by other dignitaries and various ministers and other diplomats. At 10:30AM the motorcade of President Diori arrived preceded by a large security force. On arrival, President Diori descended from the car and he was saluted by Minister Dandobi Mahamane, followed by J. A. Abbott, representing the President of the USA, Ambassador Mc Clelland and myself.

Before the cutting of the ribbon, J. A Abbott gave a speech praising the relations between the USA and the Republic of Niger and how happy the USA was to have contributed this beautiful bridge to Niger. In response, Minister Mahamane gave thanks to the USA for the bridge and praised Dr. E. Lionel Pavlo for the design of the bridge and all who have participated in its construction. It was time for the cutting of the ribbon. President Diori cut the ribbon and announced the inauguration of the bridge. The Presidential motorcade began now to cross the bridge in the sequence set by protocol, surrounded by the security. The crossing of the bridge by the motorcade went smoothly, both ways. So, I could now say, comfortably well Mission accomplished!

The Dinner

The day after the bridge ceremony, on Saturday, I left for the day with Bawa, driving into the interior. I took my camera with me and snapped many pictures of native nomads and of wild animals. We visited a market which was fascinating. Traders with camels were camped in various places with colorful textiles, and artifacts. There were storytellers recounting stories from the past, men and women dressed in traditional clothes who came to buy or sell all kinds of merchandise. I saw a lady of striking beauty and asked Bawa who it might have been. Bawa, impressed, said that she was the wife of a big chief who came to the market to buy things. It was an interesting day.

Back at the house in the evening, Antoine handed me a letter delivered by the American Embassy. It was an invitation by the President of Niger and Madame Diori Hamani to have dinner at the Palace in honor of J. A. Abbott and his wife on the 21st of December at 8:30PM. "Tenue de ville". "That is on Monday," I said to Antoine, "I must have a wellpressed shirt and my blue suit ready." I wonder who else will be there?

So on Monday evening, impeccably dressed, I drove through the gate of the Palace and as I parked the car another car pulled next to mine. It was Sarah Jane, who would also attend the dinner. We said hi! and together we walked to the entrance of the palace. At the door there was the security and a man of impressive size who escorted us through the palace stairs and then to a terrace where President and Madame Diori were sitting. Each of us went to them and paid our respects and they in turn welcomed us. I noticed that on the terrace there was security all around us, constantly watching, and I thought that the entire surrounding must have been impenetrable.

Madame Diori was wearing a large silver, silk, ceremonial dress with a white ermine cape on her shoulders and a turban covering her head of the same material as the dress. She was stunning. Sitting next to her on the same sofa was J. A. Abbott. On the next sofa was President Diori dressed in official apparel all in white, wearing a white hat sitting next to Mrs. Abbott. The floor was completely covered by a tapestry and in the center of the floor there was a table with a vase on top with flowers. The entire surrounding was regal. Sitting to the left of Madame Diori was Ambassador Mc Clelland and next to him Sarah Jane. I was sitting between a gentleman and his wife whom I had not met yet, next to Sarah Jane. We sat there conversing before going to the dining area.

At dinner the seat sequence was the same except that I sat across from Ambassador Mac Clelland. The food served was of superb quality and although the dinner was very formal it was pleasant. At the end of the dinner, J. A. Abbott read a poem by President Nixon to President Diori. It was a lovely poem and we all clapped.

We then left the table and went back to the terrace where other governmental officials had arrived and we were introduced to them. At one point one of the officials asked me how long will the bridge last and I replied, "100 years or more, and if you take care of it, another 100 years or more". Ambassador Mc Clelland having heard what I said came and whispered in my ear "You certainly did answer well". At the end of the evening we all paid respect to President and Madame Diori and left with pleasant remembrances.

On December 23 I would be visiting old friends in Venice for a week, Lucy Simonetti, Patricia and Luigi Pignatari of Rome. I would be their guest for the Christmas Holidays and then return to Niamey.

PRESIDENT NIXON'S POEM TO PRESIDENT DIORI
A PASSAGE FROM LONGFELLOW:

> Lives of great men oft remind us
> We can make our lives sublime
> And departing, leave behind us
> Footprints on the sands of time.

Haiti

On the 22 I left Niamey for Paris on Air Afrique and from Paris to Rome. In Rome I phoned Lucy and told her I was on my way and that I would be taking the Direttissimo from Rome to Milan. She told me that she would pick me up in Milano at the station and from there we would drive to Vicenza, to her home. I left Rome going North in the Direttissimo and, as always, I enjoyed the train ride. There was something special riding a long distance in a train, looking at the landscape listening to the steady rhythm of the wheels and the blowing of the whistle. It was a comfortable ride and I slept well in my sleeping cabin through the night.

In the early morning the train entered the station in Milan and I was anxious to see Lucy. And there she was with her hair blowing in the wind and as always full of enthusiasm looking for me as I was exiting the station. She immediately recognized me and we embraced. "Come" she said "I haven't seen you for such a long time and yet you still look the same". "You are even more beautiful" I said. "Since our school days I've always wanted to see you again". She looked at me and smiled with her irresistible look.

As we exited Lucy guided me to her car, a sport BMW, and said " We'll be in Vicenza very shortly". Lucy always enjoyed driving fast and soon we were there. She had a lovely home and my stay there could not have been more pleasant and relaxing. Lucy was a marvelous hostess and I must say there was nothing missing. The house help was most courteous and helpful. They all made sure that I was at all times comfortable, knowing that I was coming from a very hot region in Africa.

I stayed overnight and the next morning Lucy and I left for Venice. This time Lucy had a car with a chauffeur, so we relaxed in the back seat and chatted, reminiscing about the pleasant past and our younger years. Soon we arrived in Venice where Lucy knew everything, since she was born there. We walked crossing the old, small bridges over the canal and visited "Piazza San Marco." She showed me her old neighborhood where she grew up.

Later we went to see Patricia, her daughter and her husband Luigi at their home. They had a newborn baby and there was lots of excitement. Lucy, later in the afternoon had to go back to Vicenza and Luigi and Patricia asked me to stay with them. They both were most gracious and I had a lovely time. In the evening I invited them to go with me to the Lido's Casino to play Roulette. They were delighted to join me. We all bid good night to the baby and the Nanny and from Piazza San Marco we took a local boat and went to the Lido.

At the Casino I began playing Roulette, placing the bet on the odds when the red color came up and on the even for the black color. and I began winning. Soon Patricia and Luigi wanted to try playing and with my guidance they also began winning. They thought it was great and wondered how I came up with such an idea but I told them that it was a secret. After awhile, as always, the zero showed up and I told them to stop playing. It was a great feeling having won and so Luigi suggested we go to a discotheque in Venice and celebrate. We did and I enjoyed seeing Patricia and Luigi dancing, a young couple in love. By now it is 4AM and we decided to go home. I was happy that the evening went so well and that Patricia and Luigi had such a great time.

But my Christmas holidays had to be cut short. As I did every day, that morning I put in my call to Dr. ELP in New York and to my surprise Dr. ELP urgently asked me to come back to New York as soon as possible. I replied that although the bridge in Niamey was completed I was still needed there but, Dr. ELP replied "It is imperative that you come immediately to New York". I said I would. I phoned Lucy and told her that unexpected circumstances require my presence in New York and I must go. I told her that I had a wonderful time and I was sorry that this had to happen and that I would keep in touch and hope to see her soon again. And so, after saying goodbye to Patricia and the baby, Luigi took me to the Marco Polo Airport in Venice and on Ali Italia I left for London-New York.

A car picked me up at Kennedy Airport and drove me directly to Dr. ELP's house in the east fifties. Dr. ELP was waiting for me, and after shaking hands and with a reciprocal smile, Dr. ELP said "we will have an early dinner here at my house while I explain the nature of your assignment in Port Au Prince".

Dr. ELP's house was a duplex with a kitchen adjacent to a dining room and a library with a study above. The other floors were undoubtedly the living quarters. We were alone in the house and I was surprised to see Dr. ELP prepare our dinner in the kitchen. "In meetings like ours, I prefer to be alone" Dr. ELP says. "I hope you don't mind my cooking". I kept silent, observing and listening. We then sat at the table on which Dr. ELP had already set the dinnerware and first we had corn on the cob and after that he served leg of lamb. I must say it was delicious. I expressed my appreciation to Dr. ELP of his cuisine and told him I was now ready to hear the details of my assignment.

Dr. ELP, in a most relaxed manner, began explaining the details. "The subject of this study is the existing road connecting Port Au Prince to Leogan, the urban area of Port Au Prince and its satellite region of Carefour. This road, the only road in existence connecting the north with the south peninsula is of primary concern to the government of Haiti due to the fact that the road in question is inadequate to serve the population density concentrated in those areas, one that is continually expanding. Your assignment is to take photos of Port Au-Prince Bay and to verify some technical data of a study undertaken in 1961 by Meissner Engineering of Chicago and Utah International of a road connecting Port-Au-Prince–La Cayes. These firms supplied all technical studies of the terrain allowing the French Engineering Company Ingeroute to realize a feasibility study which includes in part the area of our project. In addition, should the government of Haiti not supply you with a helicopter to take the photos of the bay, the best location for taking such photos would be on the high hills above Port Au Prince."

After having listened attentively, I said "how much time do I have to accomplish this?" "It should not take more than a week, I estimate" Dr. ELP replied. I began folding the notes which I took while Dr. ELP was briefing me, for me to later memorize, when Dr. ELP handed me his personal camera and said "I'm sure you are familiar with this" and wished me good luck. I thanked him and assured him that I would do my best to insure a successful mission.

I arrived in Port Au Prince and one of the many private taxis waiting at the airport took me to a hotel. I signed in. I settled down in my room and began to assess the best way to do my assignment. Dr. ELP had given me a list of names to contact at the government level including Dr. Gui Noel, a personal representative of the President of Haiti, Baby Doc. But before contacting anyone I decided to take a walk and assess the environment. Poverty was very apparent as Haiti is considered one of the poorest countries in the world. Not too far from Cuba, this peninsula includes also the Dominican Republic.

While I was walking I noticed I was being followed, so I slowed down my pace for the person behind me to pass, which he did. Then he stops and asked me where I was going and how long was I to stay in Haiti. I knew then that he was a government person from security and I replied that I was in Haiti for business reasons in the construction field. He said "Bien" and then left. That reminded me of the familiar face, but then I thought Haiti is not Niger.

Back at the hotel I placed a call to Dr.Gui Noel who agreed to meet with me the next day. At the meeting, I explained to him that for our preliminary technical study we need to take photographs of the bay of Port Au Prince, and could he possibly provide us with an Army helicopter in order for us to take the photos. He replied that he would let me know. Later he called me at the hotel saying that it was with much regret that he could not supply a helicopter because of security reasons and the Army would not allow it. So, I had no other alternative but to climb high on the hill above Port-Au-Prince and take the snapshots, as Dr. Pavlo suggested. I had the feeling I was being watched and I was very careful not to be noticed when I took the shots. Fortunately, no one tried to stop me.

I now had the photos and so I could concentrate on the preliminary study of the areas and see who else was there from other parts of the world for the same purpose. Among the alternatives mentioned by Dr. Pavlo, when he briefed me, one was to build a bridge over the bay. I found out that the Germans were proposing the bridge as a project, but that was of no concern since the Haitian representatives were favoring the building of a road along the shore over the filled area of Port-Au-Prince.

And so having sufficient information and the photos of the bay I decided it was time for me to leave Haiti and return to Niamey. But before leaving, I was in my room packing my things when I noticed on the small table near the bed a red envelope addressed to my name. That reminded me of the red goat in Niamey. I opened the envelope and there was a photo of the French coast of Nice, la Cote d'Azur. The photo was labeled "The new founding of Port-Au-Prince". I began assessing the meaning of the photo and after a while I realized that there were striking similarities between the French coast of Nice and the coast of Port-Au-Prince. Thus, the photos of Nice could only suggest the development of the coast of Port-Au-Prince similar to that of Nice, thus creating a new Cote d'Azur, in Haiti. It was an appealing idea and so I decided to include it in my technical report to Dr. ELP stating: "The sponsoring of the new founding of Port-Au-Prince, which would become universally known as the new Cote d'Azur, will be the initiation of an enduring tourist boom and a major step in the elevation of Haitian economic growth from the poorest country in the western hemisphere to a financially stable Haiti by further justifying itself with the realization of an efficient road connecting the north with the south peninsula which is also so vital in this forecast of Haitian economic growth." Before leaving Paris back to Niamey, I mailed the report and all the photos to Dr. Pavlo in New York wondering what kind of reaction it would have.

The Medals

Back in Niamey I was working with Sarah Jane on quantities and extras for the last estimate to be approved for the contractor. I was spending most of my time in the office and one day Dr.E.L.P. calls me and congratulated me for the well done report on Haiti, including the photos, and told me not to forget to come back to New York.

I now had to gather all the files, from the date of the beginning of the bridge, and all the important records and ship them to the office in New York. This task would take a little time since I didn't want to miss anything. Mary Lou Harvey, the Ambassador's secretary called me on the telephone and informed me that there was an important letter for me. She would send it down. It was an invitation from Minister Dandobi Mahamane to a reception at his residence that evening, January 8, at 6:30 PM. "Tenue de ville". I called Mary Lou Harvey back to thank her and she told me that the Ambassador would also be there.

So at 6:30 I arrived at the residence of Minister Mahamane and Ambassador Mc Clelland was already there. I greeted the Minister and his wife and was curious to know of what was going on. Then Gallinari arrives with Monteil of Regie General. I went to the Ambassador and I asked him why the press was there and he finally said "you are going to be decorated". I had never been decorated before and this was definitely a new experience for me. Then the Minister calls the names of Gallinari and Monteil and asked them to come forward. Two officials of the GON were standing next to the Minister holding a plate with medals on it. Then the Minister took the medals from the plate and pinned them on Gallinari and Monteil. He made a speech and commended them as Officers of the

National Order of the Republic of Niger. A kiss on the cheek by the Minister and then we all clapped while the flashing of cameras from the press was going on.

Immediately after the Minister called my name and because I was a little nervous I was glad that Ambassador Mc Clelland was next to me. So Minister Dandobi Mahamane gave another speech and pinned on the lapel of my jacket a medal and commended me as Chevalier of the National Order of the Republic of Niger and kissed me on the cheek. The cameras were again flashing as the press was writing down the responses to their questions. Then, Gallinari, Monteil and I, shook hands with each other and the Minister. Then the Ambassador congratulated me and I could see in him a sense of relief that finally the bridge was finished and that the decoration ceremony had gone well.

The Departure

Sarah Jane and I, together with the GON, had agreed on all quantities to be paid to the contractor and, except for minor details, we were closing the books. Shortly, I would have to leave and I was anxious to go back home to the USA. Ambassador Mc Clelland had come down to my office to discuss various subjects pertaining to the Bridge and he also invited me to have a cocktail at his residence before my departure.

At the cocktail party Mrs. Mc Clelland was a gracious host and she sat next to me. There were other guests and they all asked me what I thought of the bridge. I reassured them that the bridge would be the principal factor in the future development of the other side of Niamey. There were also two F.B.I. agents stationed in Tangier, invited by the Ambassador, and I chatted with them. I told them that I did always want to see Tangier and that some day I might go there. They replied that they would be more than glad to have me there. The Ambassador and all the other guests said that they were sad to see me leave, but such is the diplomatic life when you work overseas. You get to know some one well by working together, and then you have to say goodbye.

I returned to my place and had a drink with Antoine and told him that I am leaving on the 6th of February and that he should now try to find another job. I told him that I was happy with his work that he did a good job. Bawa also was sad to see me go and I gave him the letter of reference. The day before I left I also paid my respects to President Diori and Minister Kaziende who warmly expressed their gratitude and satisfaction for all I did for Niger.

I would miss Niger, such an old land going back 600,000 years, when man began inhabiting what is now the Sahara desert of the northern part of the country. Going as far back as the Songhai empire and it's people who from the banks of the Nile in Egypt left and settled in the valley of "Joliba" later to be known as Niger. My impressions of Niger would always stay with me and I hoped one day to go back there and re-live the interesting moments of my short stay in Africa.

On the day of my departure, Sarah Jane, Emil Morin and many others who knew me, including some workers, came to the airport to say good-by and I was really touched by their warm and sincere farewell. And then as I was boarding the plane and waving goodbye to everyone, on the side of the gate, standing there was the familiar face with the Red Goat on his side, holding a sign that said in big letters: "I love you daddy". A tear came down from my eye and in return I said, "I love you daddy".

SIGNING OF NIGER BRIDGE AGREEMENT.
FROM LEFT: HARRY PELEQUIN, AID/W; SOLOM SHERMAN; USAID/NIGER
ROBERT J. RYAN, SR, AMBASSADOR TO NIGER; PRESIDENT HAMANI DIORI OF NIGER
MINISTER OF FINANCE, CUORMO; MINISTER OF AGRICULTURE , MAIDAH MAMADOU
MINISTER OF EDUCATION, HAROU KOKKA: MINISTER OF POST, MOUDDOR

FROM LEFT: PRESIDENT DIORI   DR. E. LIONEL PAVLO   PERRY HUANG

The Bridge in construction

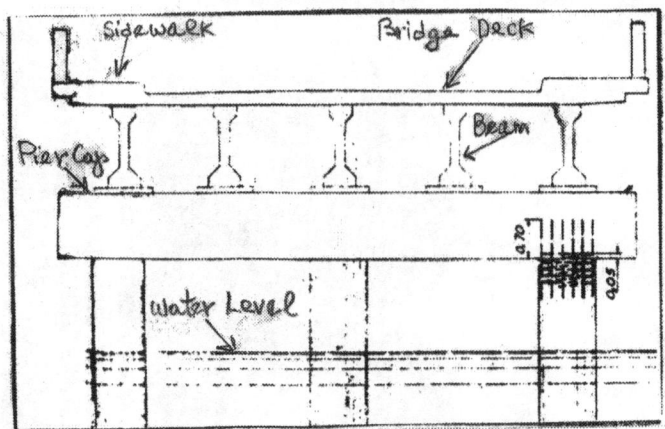

**Bridge cross section showing the beams on pier
cap supporting the bridge deck and sidewalk.**

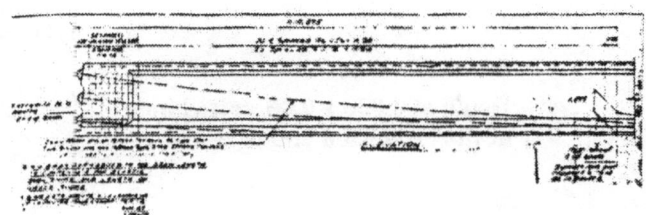

**One half of the beam showing the parabolic
curve of the three tendons, F1, F2, F3,**

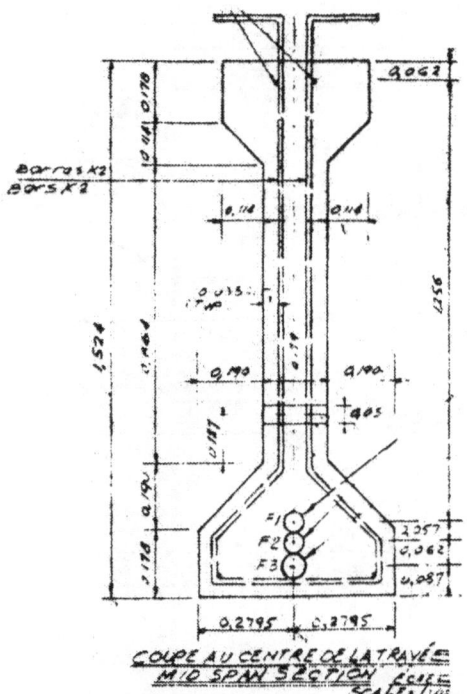

**Mid Span Section showing
the tendons, F1, F2, F3.**

Detail of 0.033 x 0.05 slotted hole
at the expansion end of beam.

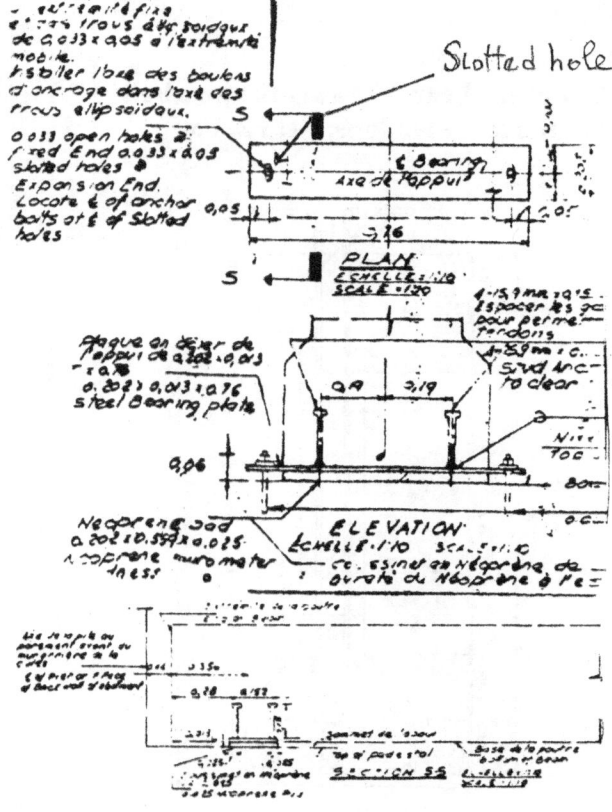

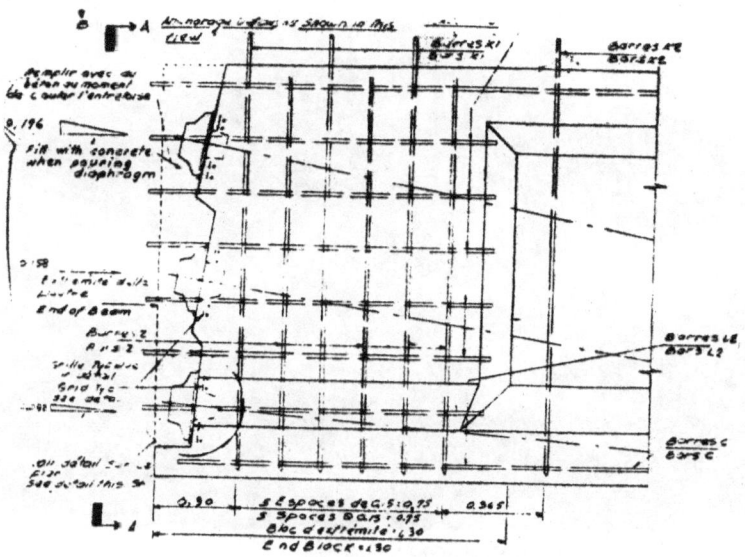

Tendons detail at end of beam.

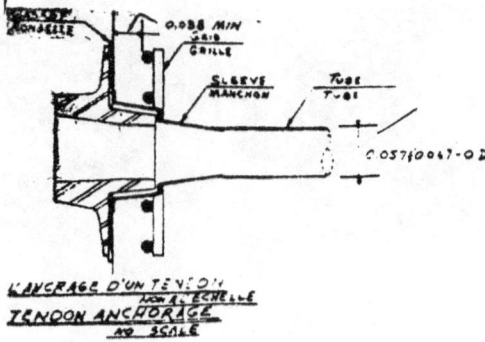

The field office of the bridge.

One of the Abutment of the bridge.

Remo Capra Bloise waiting for President Diori to arrive.

RS/R FILES

Attention _____
Keep this study together.

DEC 10 1970

MEMORANDUM FOR THE PRESIDENT

Subject: United States Delegation to
Attend National Day ceremonies
of the Republic of Niger

This Government has accepted the invitation of
the Government of the Republic of Niger to be represented at the ceremonies commemorating the tenth
anniversary of the independence of the Republic of
Niger, the twelfth anniversary of the proclamation
of the Republic, and the dedication of the John F.
Kennedy Bridge, which are to be held at Niamey on
December 18, 1970.

To head the United States Delegation at these
ceremonies, I recommend that John Adams Abbott, the
oldest living male descendant of the presidential
Adams family and a psychiatrist, be designated your
Personal Representative, with the rank of Special
Ambassador. I also recommend that Roswell D.
McClelland, American Ambassador to the Republic of
Niger, be designated your Personal Representative,
with the rank of Special Ambassador, at these cere-
monies.

There are enclosed for your approval letters
accrediting your Personal Representatives in the
capacities indicated.

/s/ William P. Rogers

William P. Rogers

Enclosures:

Letters of credence (2).

DG/PAS/PC:BFSheskin   O/DG   S/CR   AF/W   AF   S/S
12-9-70

POL 17-4 NIGER XR POL 7 US/ABBOTT

RICHARD NIXON

PRESIDENT OF THE UNITED STATES OF AMERICA

To His Excellency

Hamani Diori,

President of the Republic of Niger.

Excellency:

Desiring to give evidence of my appreciation of the cordial relations existing between the United States of America and the Republic of Niger, I have designated John Adams Abbott as my Personal Representative, with the rank of Special Ambassador, to attend the ceremonies commemorating the tenth anniversary of the independence of the Republic of Niger, the twelfth anniversary of the proclamation of the Republic, and the dedication of the John F. Kennedy Bridge.

I have entire confidence that Dr. Abbott will be acceptable to you in the distinguished duty with which I have invested him.

I therefore ask that you receive my Personal Representative favorably and accept from him the renewed assurances of my high regard and of the friendship which he bears of the Government and people of the United States of America for you and the Government and people of the Republic of Niger.

Very truly yours,

By the President: /s/ Richard Nixon

/s/ William P. Rogers

Secretary of State.

Washington, December 12, 1970
DG/PAS/PC:SFSRankin
12-9-70   O/DG   S/CPR   AF/W   AF   S/S-S

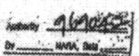

LIMITED OFFICIAL USE
Classification DEC 7 '70 22   41   203761

Department of State

TELEGRAM

POL 17-4 NIGER
POL 33-1 NIGER RIV.

INDICATE:
☐ COLLECT
☐ CHARGE TO

DISTRIBUTION

ACTION: Amembassy NIAMEY

Subject: December 18 ceremonies

REF: State 203017

1. Dept proposes Dr. Abbott deliver following speech in French at bridge dedication:

Mr. President of the Republic, Distinguished Guests: I am deeply honored to be in Niamey today for this celebration of Republic Day. This is the first trip my wife and I have made to Africa, and I must say how impressed I have been during my short visit here with the warmth and friendliness of the people of Niger.

President Nixon, who asked me to represent him personally at today's ceremonies, requested that I transmit this message from him to your distinguished President.

QUOTE: Dear Mr. President: As your country celebrates this ~~important~~ significant National Day, allow me to express my congratulations and those of the Government and people of the United States. I have been impressed by your country's development efforts ~~of its own resources~~ and am most pleased that the United States has been able to assist with the important bridge being

DRAFTED BY:
AF/W:CHTwining:lw

DRAFTING DATE: 12/11/70

TEL. EXT.: 20842

APPROVED BY:
AF - W. Beverly Carter, Jr.

CLEARANCES:
AF/W - Mr. Aggrey   S/S - Mr. Curran

Text received from White House

LIMITED OFFICIAL USE

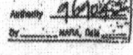

Department of State
TELEGRAM

INDICATE:
☐ COLLECT
☐ CHARGE TO

DISTRIBUTION

ACTION: Amembassy NIAMEY   PAGE 2

dedicated on this day. I wish you continued success in
your wise leadership of the Republic of Niger, and I hope
that the already close relations between our two countries
will continue to be strengthened. RICHARD M. NIXON. UNQTE.

Mr. President, the United States is proud of the
mutual friendship and respect on which our relations are
based. In addition, my country has long admired your wise
leadership in international affairs and commends your
initiatives aimed at increasing regional cooperation in
Africa. We consider that this bridge serves both as a
reminder of the friendship between us and a demonstration
of your own interest in the development of your country
and in your ties with your neighbors.

The United States is most honored by your naming this
bridge after the late John F. Kennedy. The late President
was very interested in this project, as you know. He did
not dream the bridge would one day bear his name, but when
our two governments first began discussing the project

DRAFTED BY:

CLEARANCES:

DRAFTING DATE TEL. EXT. APPROVED BY:

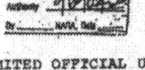

LIMITED OFFICIAL USE
Classification

Department of State

TELEGRAM

INDICATE:
☐ COLLECT
☐ CHARGE TO

DISTRIBUTION

ACTION: Amembassy NIAMEY   PAGE 3

        the
in/early 1960's, President Kennedy realized its importance
for the people of Niger. President Johnson and President
Nixon have remained interested in the completion of this
project. It is a mark of President Nixon's own interest
that he asked me to represent him today.

      On behalf of the Government and people of the United
States, allow me to express my hope that your country will
continue to know success in its efforts to modernize. Thank
you so much for inviting me here today. May this bridge
we are dedicating, bearing the name of the late John
Fitzgerald Kennedy and expressing the interest of the United
States of America in the Republic of Niger, serve for future
generations as an example of friendship, progress, and
peace. Thank you.

DRAFTED BY:

CLEARANCES:

DRAFTING DATE | TEL. EXT. | APPROVED BY:

LIMITED OFFICIAL USE
Classification

FORM DS-322

UNCLASSIFIED 707 22   20   20292

Classification

Department of State   POL 17-4 NIGER
                                       POL 33-1 NIGER RIVER
TELEGRAM   &   * POL 7 US/ABBOTT

INDICATE:
☐ COLLECT
☐ CHARGE TO

DISTRIBUTION

ACTION: Amembassy NIAMEY PRIORITY

SUBJECT: December 18 Ceremonies

1. Designation Dr. Abbott and Amb. McClelland as Personal
Representatives of Pres Nixon announced White House press
briefing A.M. Dec. 14. You now authorized publicize Abbott
attendance, as desired.

2. Senator Kennedy's letter will be hand carried by Abbott.
Text follows:

Dear Mr. President:

I wanted to write you this personal letter to assure
you and the people of the Republic of Niger how deeply honored
the Kennedy family is that the great new bridge spanning
the Niger River will be named in memory of President Kennedy.

On many occasions during his term in office, President
Kennedy proclaimed his deep interest in -- and his abiding
respect for -- the people of African nations. In 1963, he
said qte I think that history will record this past decade in
Africa as one of the most astonishing bursts of human energy,
human initiative, and responsibility that the world has ever

DRAFTED BY:
AF/W:CHTwining:iw

DRAFTING DATE TEL. EXT. APPROVED BY:
12/14/70   20842   AF/W - O. Rudolph Aggrey

CLEARANCES:
DG/PAS - Mrs. Remo (subst.)
H - Mr. Samuels (subst.)

FORM DS-322
4 - 65

UNCLASSIFIED
Classification

UNCLASSIFIED
Classification

Department of State

TELEGRAM

INDICATE:
☐ COLLECT
☐ CHARGE TO

DISTRIBUTION

ACTION: Amembassy NIAMEY   PAGE 2

   end qte
known/. These words have additional meaning in 1970 for
your country as you celebrate your Republic's first decade
of independence.

   I sincerely regret that I am not able to be with you
on December 18th -- an important milestone for your country
and a meaningful occasion for the Kennedy family. We express
our gratitude to you and your Government for this significant
tribute to President Kennedy. Sincerely, EDWARD M. KENNEDY

                             ROGERS

DRAFTED BY: DRAFTING DATE | TEL. EXT. | APPROVED BY:

CLEARANCES:

FORM DS-322
4-68

UNCLASSIFIED
Classification

The Plaque.

The arrival of President Diori at the bridge.

From left: Ambassador Mc Clelland; The Minister of Transport of Niger;
Mrs. Mc Clelland; Ambassador Ryan; Remo Capra Bloise.

J.A.Abbott and President Diori cutting the ribbon at the opening of the bridge.

From left: Madame Diori; President Nixon representative, J.A.Abbott; President Diori and Mrs. Abbott.

From left: Official of A.I.D.; Remo Capra Bloise; wife of the A.I.D. official; Sarah Jane Littlefield; Ambassador Roswell D. Mc Clelland.

A section of the bridge.

Remo Capra Bloise   Minister   Dandobi Mahamane

President Diori with President Johnson at the White House reviewing the Guards of Honor

About the Author

Remo Capra Bloise is a member of the American Society of Composers and Authors (ASCAP). He has previously written a drama, *The Cube*, and a musical, *Sword of Fire*.

As a construction engineer, he has worked in Manhattan in many projects, including the rock excavation and foundation for the Corning Glass Building at 56th St. and Fifth Ave., and the foundation for the 107th Regiment Infantry Memorial Monument on 67th and Fifth. He is a member of the International Union of Operating Engineers "I.U.O.E.", Local 15D, the surveyors' division.

He also recorded an album of American popular standards for Columbia Records that is now distributed as a CD by Sony Music Special Products.

0-595-00694-9